CLASSIC I
NUMBER C

MW00709499

NEW JERSEY CRAGS

by
Paul Nick
and
Neil J.A. Sloane

Chockstone Press
Evergreen, Colorado
1996

Classic Rock Climbs: New Jersey Crags

Cover photo of Paul Nick on The Prow, Bear Rock, Pyramid Mountain, taken by Ruthanne Wagner.

ISBN: 1-57540-025-1 *Classic Rock Climbs* series
         1-57540-032-4 *New Jersey Crags*

Published and distributed by:
Chockstone Press, Inc.
Post Office Box 3505
Evergreen, CO 80437-3505

DEDICATION

This book is dedicated to the memory of two of the most amazing climbers of all time:

Wolfgang Güllich (1960–1992) and Derek Hersey (1957–1993)

Anyone who was fortunate enough to share a rope or a beer with them became a better climber. Two quotes:

Derek Hersey, to someone starting a route:

 "Remember, when in doubt, run it out."

Ron Fawcett, being interviewed by the German climbing magazine *Rotpunkt* on the anniversary of his first ascent of *The Master's Edge:*

 "Was möchtest Du besitzen?" [What would you wish for?]
 "Was Wolfgang hat." [What Wolfgang has.]

All royalties from the sale of this book will be donated to The Access Fund.

ACKNOWLEDGMENTS

Without the help of the following people, this guide would be a fraction of its current size. John Anderson placed at our disposal his vast storehouse of information on climbing and nature areas in New Jersey. John is primarily responsible for saving the Cradle Rock area from development. Doug Auld told us about the Hemlock Falls Area. Ted Cais told us about Jenny Jump and several bouldering areas he discovered. Harry Drechsel supplied information about climbs in Norvin Green State Forest. Andrew and Jason Kondracki provided us with descriptions of several climbing areas. Lyle Lange provided helpful information about several areas and was a valuable source of information about legal and access issues. Lyle, the director of Mountain Sports AdventureSchool, has been working to change state laws so that climbing is recognized as a legitimate use of New Jersey state parks. John McEldowney produced a short list of New Jersey climbs in the early 1980s, and was the coauthor with Neil Sloane of an unpublished 1988 version of this guide.

Steve O'Keefe gave us permission to use the material in his guidebook to Green Pond. Steve also provided us with descriptions of the climbing at Garret Mountain, Rifle Camp and other areas. Marc Ronca made up the recommended route list for Mt. Minsi at the Delaware Water Gap. Dave Ryan sent us a description of the climbs at Mills Reservation. Richard Scheuer supplied information about climbs at Waterloo Rocks. Mike Siaca told us about the Norvin Green State Forest area and the Ringwood cliffs. Ed Walters sent us a detailed guide to the climbs at Cranberry Ledges. Unfortunately the latter are on private property, and have therefore not been included.

We would also like to thank the following, who made valuable suggestions or comments: Doug Allcock, Douglass Bell, Vic Benes, Susanna Cuyler, Bill Danna, Jack Davis, Mike Flood, Mark Fordeney, Jeff Gruenberg, Bob Kurshan, Robert McClellan, Jack Mileski, Greg Perkins, Russ Raffa, Todd Ritter, Michael Schlaugh, Ronald Sloane, Mike Steele and Paul Tukey.

PREFACE

A climbing guide to New Jersey? As likely as a deep-sea fishing guide to Nebraska, you say? Not so! Scattered throughout the Garden State are a number of worthwhile cliffs, outcrops and boulders. This first-of-a-kind guide presents you with a surprising abundance of multipitch traditional routes, heinous boulder problems, bolted faces and toprope lines located throughout central and northern New Jersey, and just over the state's borders. Some big-name climbers have trained on the rock described in these pages: Henry Barber, Jeff Gruenberg, Lynn Hill, Colin Lanz, Russ Raffa, William Shockley and many others.

This guide will be useful if :

- you are a New Jersey climber interested in new areas;
- you are bored with your local climbing gym;
- you live elsewhere but sometimes visit your aunt in Short Hills—this could make those visits just a bit more enjoyable; or
- you are driving from Washington to New Hampshire and would like to break the trip to sample some New Jersey classics.

Well, that's the sales pitch! No preface would be complete, however, without some kind of justification. There are good reasons both for and against publishing a guidebook such as this. In recent years the dramatic number of new climbers has created overuse and overcrowding problems at a few well-known crags, especially the Shawangunks, Ralph Stover State Park and Allamuchy State Park. It would be unfortunate if this guidebook simply extended these problems to every area in the state. It is our hope that this guidebook will mitigate these problems through a "spread-the-wealth" effect in which climbers realize they can meet their recreational needs closer to home. Curiously, more than one climber implored us not to include the crag nearest his home but urged us to include the other areas.

This guide should not be interpreted as a recommendation to climb at the places described or that climbing is permitted at these places. It is rather a description of areas where people have climbed in the past and where hopefully climbing will be done at some future and happier time when there are fewer restrictions.

Our intent was to include only climbing areas located on public land, on private property where climbing is permitted, or on private property earmarked for public acquisition. If we have mistakenly included any climbs on private land, please let us know and we will remove the area from the next edition.

TABLE OF CONTENTS

INTRODUCTION 1

CHAPTER 1: MERCER COUNTY 5
Mt Rose (cradle Rock) 5

CHAPTER 2: HUNTERDON COUNTY 17
Sourland Mountain Reservoir 17
Buzzard's Butte 19
Reigelsville CLiffs 20
Musconetcong Gorge Nature Preserve 22
Teetertown Nature Preserve 26

CHAPTER 3: WARREN COUNTY 29
Jenny Jump State Forest 29
Delaware Water Gap 31
Ricks Rocks 41

CHAPTER 4: SUSSEX COUNTY 43
Allamuchy State Park (Waterloo Rocks) 43
High Point State Park 49

CHAPTER 5: MORRIS COUNTY 51
Green Pond 51
Pyramid Mountain Park 61
Tourne County Park (The Tourne) 63

CHAPTER 6: PASSAIC COUNTY 69
Norvin Green State Forest (Pine Paddies) 69
Garrent Mountain Reservation 76
Rifle Camp Park 79

CHAPTER 7: ESSEX COUNTY 83
Mills Reservation 83
South Mountain Rservation 86
   Hemlock Falls 86
   Turtle Back Rock 87

CHAPTER 8: UNION COUNTY 93
Watchung Reservation (Seeley's Escarpment) 93

CHAPTER 9: OTHER NEW JERSEY AREAS 101

CHAPTER 10: MANHATTAN 105

INDEX 109

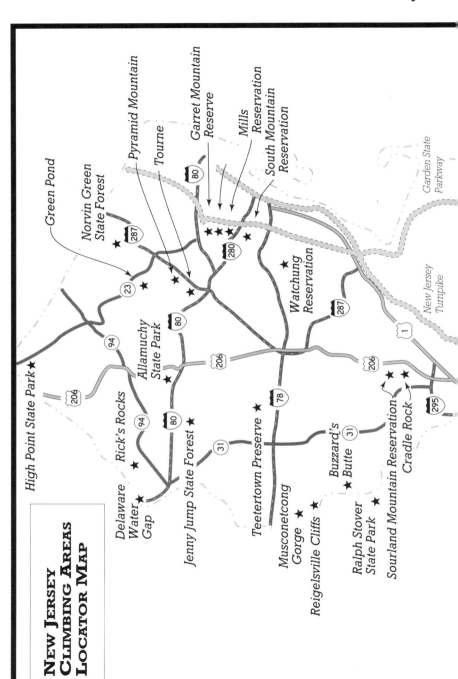

NEW JERSEY
CLIMBING AREAS
LOCATOR MAP

High Point State Park ★

Green Pond

Norvin Green State Forest

Pyramid Mountain

Tourne

Garret Mountain Reserve

Mills Reservation

South Mountain Reservation

Watchung Reservation

Garden State Parkway

New Jersey Turnpike

Allamuchy State Park

Rick's Rocks

Delaware Water Gap

Jenny Jump State Forest

Teetertown Preserve ★

Musconetcong Gorge ★

Reigelsville Cliffs ★

Buzzard's Butte ★

Ralph Stover State Park ★

Sourland Mountain Reservation

Cradle Rock

INTRODUCTION

NEW JERSEY

This guidebook is a comprehensive source of information on climbing areas in New Jersey. It is divided into chapters according to county, and the counties are arranged in roughly clockwise order beginning with Mercer County. A few of the areas are located just outside the borders of New Jersey. Our rationale for including such areas is that any rock within a short drive of the state's borders is essentially a local resource for New Jersey climbers. Our original plan was to include Raph Stover in this book, since most NJ climbers regard those cliffs as part of greater New Jersey. Just as the best climbing in Holland is just over the border in Belgium, some of the best climbing in New Jersey is just across the river in Pennsylvania! However, in order to comply with the constraints of this series of guides, it has been necessary to split off the Ralph Stover section as a separate book – Volume 12 of this series.

Within the guide itself, each climbing area is introduced with a three-line heading that gives the name, the location, and a brief description of the area. The brief description gives the height and type of rock as well as the nature and difficulty of the climbing. The phrase "Local Interest" is a disclaimer indicating that you may be disappointed if you spend more than a half-hour getting there.

Since this is the first guidebook for New Jersey, it may be more subject to error than other guides. Some of the information has been contributed by other people, and has not been checked by the authors. Furthermore, conditions can change rapidly in this state. Rocks that were hidden in a forest one year may be in someone's backyard the next. If you discover any inaccuracies or omissions, please let us know by writing to us in care of the publisher.

One or more of the following sections are provided for each climbing area:

ACCESS ISSUES This section gives any information known to the authors at the time of writing about the permissibility of climbing in the area. Such information is not guaranteed to be accurate and complete either before or after the publication date. Regardless of such information, you must take full responsibility for your own actions. This book does not give you a license to climb in any area. You must determine whether climbing is permitted and you must use discretion and responsible judgment.

Four of the areas in this guide are in New Jersey state parks. A special-use permit is presently required to climb in these areas. We are told that in the past such permits have been issued only to commercial guiding services. However, in 1996 the New Jersey state park administrative code will come under review. This presents an excellent opportunity to make the code more favorable to individual climbers (who after all vote and pay taxes just like other recreational users!). Since this opportunity will not come again this century, we recommend writing a letter to your local politicians (freeholders, congresspersons, senators) and to the Director of New Jersey State Park Services, CN404, Trenton, NJ 08625, urging that climbing be recognized as a legitimate use of state parks.

Most of the other areas in this guide, located in nature preserves and county parks, do not have an explicit access policy. Also, as most climbers are aware, explicit policy, where it exists, is subject to change at any time. All climbers are urged to support the Access Fund.

CLIMBING HISTORY　　We have been able to discover the climbing history of only a few of these areas. If any reader can supply us with further information, we will include it in the next edition. First ascent information, where available, is provided using the following abbreviations:

FA	First ascent	FKA	First known ascent
FFA	First free ascent	FTR	First known toprope ascent

Other abbreviations that have been used are: GSP (for the Garde State Parkway), NJT (for the New Jersey Turnpike), and PN and NJAS (for the authors).

DIRECTIONS　　Directions are given from a nearby major highway. Distances that we specifically measured with an odometer are given with a decimal point (e.g., 6.0M). Estimated distances are given as fractions. County maps will be helpful in locating these crags, and for this reason we always indicate which county a crag is in.

HAZARDS　　This section lists nasty things you may encounter such as poison ivy, blackflies, glass shard sprinkled holds, crack dealers, loose rock, horrendous landings, toxic waste, etc. We recommend that you inspect your body for ticks after visiting any of the wooded areas. Also, bring a first aid kit.

RECOMMENDED ROUTES　　A short list of the best climbs for toproping, leading and bouldering has been provided for the larger areas.

THE CLIMBING　　Routes and boulder problems are described in this section. Whenever possible, local or traditional route names have been included. In other cases, routes have been assigned names by the authors or left unnamed.

We have used a star rating system to indicate the quality of routes and boulder problems:

★   Worth doing
★★   Well worth doing
★★★ Genuine New Jersey classic

RATINGS   Routes have been graded using the modern Yosemite system with a,b,c,d extensions for routes 5.10 and harder and +,– extensions for routes easier than 5.10. A single question mark (e.g., 5.11?) indicates that the authors have not verified the grade, although it is probably close to the mark. A double question mark (e.g., 5.15a??) indicates a wild guess. A split grade (e.g.,5.10d/11a) indicates that the difficulty is highly dependent on your height, the exact line you follow or some other factor.

For many leadable routes, a protection rating has been indicated as follows:

G	Excellent protection	R	Poor/unreasonable protection
PG	Reasonable protection	X	Skull and crossbones
TR	Toprope		

You should toprope X-rated routes unless you are an Immortal. Protection ratings are merely an indication to assist you in deciding whether to even consider leading the route. It is still up to you to size up the route and decide for yourself whether you have the necessary skill and experience both at climbing and at placing protection to safely lead the route.

BOULDER PROBLEMS   A ''boulder problem'' is generally a short, difficult sequence of moves performed reasonably near the ground thereby liberating the boulderer from rope, gear and belayer. The wise boulderer always uses an alert and competent spotter, especially when the landing area contains rocks or other obstructions.

Boulder problems have been graded using the Hueco Tanks V-rating system, which starts at V0 and increases in an open-ended fashion (V0, V1, V2, etc.) Plus/minus extensions further pinpoint the difficulty. Under this system, boulder problems are graded by comparing their difficulty with that of standard-setting problems at Hueco Tanks. Each rating on the V-scale is associated with one or two specific problems that define the difficulty for that rating. Since these standard problems are in Texas, a loose translation is provided here.

V-Rating	*Yosemite Rating*
V0–, V0, V0+	5.7 to about 5.10a
V1	solid 5.10
V2 , V3	5.11
V4, V5, V6	5.12
V7, V8, V9	5.13
V10, V11...	5.14

Problems in this guidebook range from V0- to V6. To put this in perspective, the hardest problem in America (located at Hueco Tanks) is rated V13.

Boulder problems, by definition, are difficult and every fall is a ground-fall, so in some cases the guide may recommend the use of a spotter or a toprope. Some problems have been given an R or X danger rating to warn of the potential for a particularly injurious landing or long fall, sometimes in combination with loose or friable rock or tenuous or difficult moves high off the ground. R-rated problems should be toproped or otherwise attempted only by accomplished boulderers who can complete the problem with no chance of a fall. X-rated problems should only be toproped. Regardless of what the guide suggests, it is your sole responsibility to study the problem and determine the conditions under which you can attempt the problem safely, if at all. If you have any doubts, either do not attempt the problem or use a toprope.

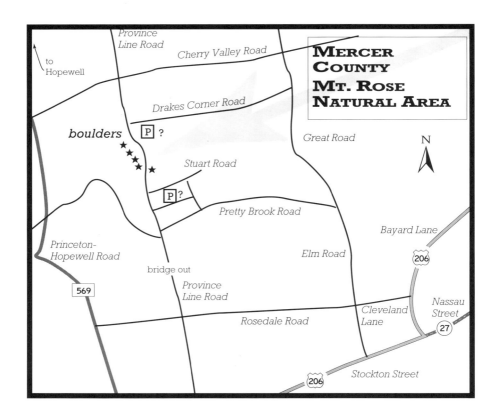

CHAPTER 1

MERCER COUNTY

MT. ROSE NATURAL AREA (CRADLE ROCK)
Near Princeton
Granite boulders; 62 problems V0–V6; Best bouldering in New Jersey

Numerous granite boulders in a wooded area on the outskirts of Princeton. This is the most extensive bouldering area in New Jersey. The climbing is mostly on thin slabs and faces, but a few steep cracks and bulges add variety. A hard bouldering session here will strip every layer of skin off your fingertips. If you wish to develop tough callouses, this area will certainly do the trick (planning a trip to Hueco Tanks?). Cradle Rock is the only area in New Jersey given a chapter in John Sherman's historical guide to bouldering, *Stone Crusade.*

ACCESS ISSUES Important! Cradle Rock is on private land. Although plans exist for Cradle Rock to be purchased as the Mount Rose Natural Area, it is still privately owned. Recently, there was an incident in which someone chopped up a dead tree leaning against one of the boulders and left the logs strewn about. The landowner was furious and only the deft political skills of John Anderson defused the situation. If you find yourself at these boulders, it is absolutely critical that you limit your environmental alterations to removing broken beer bottles and other garbage left by the partying derelicts who desecrate the area on occasion. In this way, you can make a positive impact and help maintain the goodwill of the landowners.

HISTORY A typewritten guide circulated in the 1970s by Robert Palais and Mark Sonenfeld sheds light on the early climbing activity and route development in the area. Palais started climbing here in the 1960s and cites evidence that people had climbed the boulders as early as the 1930s. Most of the problems listed in this chapter were established by Palais along with Jeff Achey and Doug Gray. Henry Barber also came by and contributed Close Shave. The reader may recognize some of these names as having played important roles in the development of climbing in the Northeast (see *Yankee Rock & Ice,* by Laura and Guy Waterman, Stackpole Books, 1993).

In the late 1980s, the Elizabethtown Water Company planned to level the area and build a 14.3-million-gallon underground water storage tank on the site. Local climbers, John Anderson ("Climber Profile: John Anderson, R.N.," *Access Notes* [newsletter of the Access Fund], Volume 4, Summer 1992) and Chris Spatz, having learned of the impending destruction of the boulder field, joined forces with local landowners, environmental groups and the Access Fund to save the area. At one point, Anderson brought a girl scout troop into the woods to introduce them to the ecology of the area, and then urged them to join the letter-writing campaign! In July 1992, the water company switched its planned site to an area 2 miles away. In June 1994, the Green Acres Program agreed to allocate a $500,000 matching grant to purchase the 128-acre tract of land surrounding the boulders ("John Anderson and the Campaign to Save Cradle Rock, NJ," *Crux Northeast* April/May 1995).

DIRECTIONS   Going south on Rt 27 (Nassau Street) in Princeton, turn right onto Rt 206 (Bayard Lane) at the War Memorial and take the third left turn onto Cleveland Lane. After 0.5 mile, turn right onto Elm Road and follow this for 0.75 mile to a left turn onto Pretty Brook Road. After 1.7 miles this turns into a T-junction with Province Line Road. Turn right. After a third of a mile, Province Line Road becomes a dirt road, just beyond Stuart Road. The boulders begin in the woods on the left side of the dirt road.

PARKING   In the past, people have parked on the south side of Stuart Road where there is room for no more than three vehicles (see figure). Under no circumstances should you park on Province Line Road or in anyone's driveway. More secluded parking is available by approaching the boulder field along Province Line Road from the north (see map below), but a rugged vehicle is needed to make it through the swampy dirt road.

HAZARDS   Many of the landings below the boulder problems are exciting. Sharp rocks, glass, tree roots and sloping ground can claim the ankles, head or spine of the careless boulderer. There are many deer in the Princeton area, and where there are deer, there are deer ticks, the carriers of the dreaded Lyme disease. If you want to catch it, this is a good place.

RECOMMENDED ROUTES   *I-54* (V0), *Granite Enema* (V0), *The Nose* (V0+), *Burt & Carole* (V1- R), *Slapping the Pig's Genitals* (V1), *Repetition* (V1+), *Thinner* (V2), *Static Cling* (V2), *Fusion Boots* (V6).

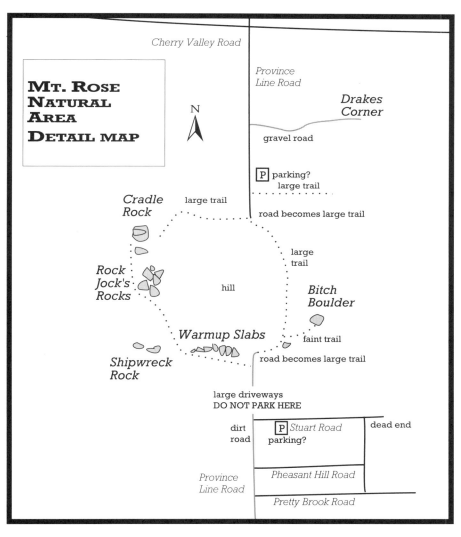

Cherry Valley Road

**MT. ROSE
NATURAL
AREA
DETAIL MAP**

Province
Line Road

N

Drakes
Corner

gravel road

P parking?
large trail

Cradle
Rock

large trail

road becomes large trail

large
trail

Rock
Jock's
Rocks

hill

Bitch
Boulder

Warmup Slabs

faint trail

road becomes large trail

Shipwreck
Rock

large driveways
DO NOT PARK HERE

dirt
road

P Stuart Road

dead end

parking?

Province
Line Road

Pheasant Hill Road

Pretty Brook Road

THE CLIMBING   Although locals claim there are over 200 boulder problems in the area, we have included only easily described, noncontrived problems. Although we have included some first ascent information, we have given only secondary consideration to maintaining the strict historical integrity of the original routes. Some climbers may look at these boulders and find the concept of a first ascent rather amusing, perhaps with justification. Nevertheless, we have included first ascent information when available.

THE WARMUP SLABS (V0–V4)

Most popular boulders in area.

1   **Lunger's Delight (V0–)**   Start on right side of boulder with palms on friction slope. Move left and up to top. 9 feet.

2   **Toe Dance (V0)**   Climb left side of boulder without touching next boulder to left. 12 feet.

3   **The Warmup Route (V0–)**   Right side of slab. Easy. 15 feet.

4   **The Burnout Route (V0–)**   Left side of slab. 15 feet.

5   **The Natural Chockstone (V0–)**   Climb absurdly easy chimney past chockstone. 14 feet.

6   **The Inverted Arrowhead (V2)**   Awkward start. Even slightest contact with boulder on left diminishes difficulty (avoiding such contact is crux). 13 feet.

7   **Route One (V0–/V0)**   Right side of slab. Hardest variation avoids right edge of boulder and big hold on upper-middle part of slab. 15 feet.

8   **I-54 (V0)** ★   Center of slab. Nice slab climbing! Slightly harder and bolder if big hold on upper-middle part of slab is not used. For additional excitement, try using palms of hands only. 15 feet.

9   **Awkward Hawk (V0–)** ★   Climb left side of slab avoiding big hold on upper-middle part of slab. "Elegant Hawk" would be a more appropriate name. 15 feet. FA: Doug Gray, Jeff Achey.

10   **March of the Republicans (V0)**   Climb boulder up in gap without using nearby boulders (except as a safety net). 12 feet.

11   **Landed Fish (V0+/V1)**   Slap your hands on top of the boulder, belly-flop over the top and writhe like a landed fish. Arête to left is off-route. Height dependent. 10 feet.

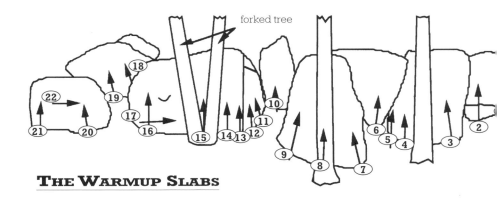

THE WARMUP SLABS

12 **Robbie's Route (V0)** Climb right side of arête finishing with scary mantle. 10 feet. FA: Robert Palais.

13 **The Nose (V0+)** ★ Left side of arête. 11 feet. FA: Doug Gray.

14 **Thinner (V2)** ★ Climb thin face just left of arête without touching arête. A fingery challenge! 12 feet.

15 **Peace Sign (V0/V2)** Many variations behind forked tree (the peace sign graffiti is no longer legible). Easiest variation starts behind left fork of tree. Hardest variation starts behind right fork of tree directly below vertical seam (straight up seam to flake, then to top). 11 to 12 feet. FA: Doug Gray.

16 **Singer (V0)** Many variations near left end of boulder. "Singer" refers to knee injury you could sustain if your feet slip off the time bomb footholds. 10 to 11 feet.

17 **Shredder (V4)** Begin standing on 2-foot-diameter rock embedded in ground below left end of boulder. Step across to boulder and perform low traverse (just above ground) to arête on right end. Sequential moves along relentless series of harsh fingertip edges and time-bomb footholds. Unpleasant! 16 feet.

18 **Shock The Monkey (V0)** Surmount undercut start to gain slab. Use only thin holds on face and avoid easy layback on right. 10 feet.

19 **Doug's Roof (V2)** ★ Short but tough overhang just right of shorter boulder (which is off-route). Harder if you can't reach starting holds from ground. For more challenge, do initial fingertip pullup and lunge with feet dangling. 9 feet. FA: Doug Gray.

20 **(V0–)** Up short boulder on right side. 9 feet.

21 **(V0–)** Up short boulder on left side. 9 feet.

22 **(V0+)** Traverse short boulder from left to right. 11 feet.

SHIPWRECK ROCK (V0–V?)

About 120 feet west of The Warmup Slabs and 100 feet south of Rock Jock's Rocks is an obscure boulder resembling the hull and prow of a ship that has come to rest in the dried-up streambed here.

23 **(V0–)** Far right end of overhanging hull. 12 feet.

24 **Project (V??)** Climb overhanging hull away from left and right ends. Desperate.

25 **Project (V??)** Hand traverse using small holds along lip of overhanging hull. Also desperate.

26 **(V0–)** Far left end of overhanging hull. 10 feet.

27   (V0)   About 30 feet west of Shipwreck Rock is a boulder with a
      tree growing against it. Climb steep face on right side of tree.
      Avoid cheatstones. Several variations possible. 11 feet.

ROCK JOCK'S ROCKS (V0–V3)

*Two large boulders next to many lesser boulders, located halfway between
the Warmup Slabs and Cradle Rock. The climbing ranges from delicate
friction slabs to gymnastic vertical faces. Birch's Tooth is the striking pyramid-
shaped boulder with slabs on the back and a steep concave face on the front.
Warning: Some of the problems in this area have truly diabolical landings.*

*(NJAS: In the spring of 1983, a climbing seminar regularly met here after
Professor Serre's number theory seminar at the Institute for Advanced Study,
usually Jean-Pierre Serre, Chair d'Algèbre et Géomètrie, Collège de France;
Bryan Birch, Oxford University; Jack Milnor, Institute for Advanced Study; and
myself. One day, Bryan Birch cried out from the top of the slab, ''Don't move!''
We looked around, expecting to see a snake, but in fact his false tooth had
popped out at the crux, and had fallen into the leaves at the base of the
boulder. We searched for days but never found it. As far as we know, it's still
there.)*

28   **Almost a Problem (V0)**   Start below dark green, lichen-covered
      face, just left of where end of smaller boulder touches it. A few
      delicate moves allow you to reach a thin hold about 2 feet from top.
      At this point, the smaller boulder can't be avoided, so do a quick
      stepup on it to reach the top. 14 feet.

29   **Peek-a-Boo (V0–)**   Start at left edge of dark-green face, just right
      and around corner from slab with D.F.S. graffiti. Climb right side of
      arête until lack of holds forces you onto left side. 15 feet.

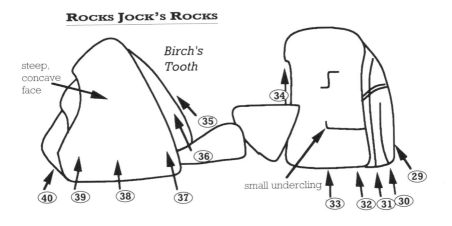

ROCKS JOCK'S ROCKS

Birch's
Tooth

steep,
concave
face

small undercling

30   **Nursery Clyme (V0–)**   Climb narrow slab at D.F.S. graffiti using only holds on slab. 16 feet.

31   **Down By The Corner (V0–)**   Start in small corner and finish up on left. Absurdly easy. 18 feet.

32   **Romparête (V0+)** ★   Straddle arête to top. Feet should stay at least 1 foot away from easy ramps on right side. 18 feet.

33   **Finger Gripping Good (V2/V3)** ★   Start at small undercling and climb center of face to top. The V3 version, best done using a toprope, completely avoids left and right outside corners (including tempting small flake on right-hand corner). Easier variations use the left or right corner, but only after good holds halfway up the boulder have been reached. 18 feet. FA: Doug Gray.

34   **Mission Control (V2)**   Launching pad is at entrance to chimney/cave hidden in cramped spot around corner from Finger Gripping Good. Start on right side of outside corner (short, overhanging, obtuse angle) with left hand on good flake. Crank up and right (long reach) and clear small overhang above (scary mantle). Nearby boulders off-route. Spotter recommended. The final mantle can be done as a problem in itself by stemming over from nearby boulder (High Test V0+). 14 feet. FA: Doug Gray.

35   **Pyramid of Friction (V0– R)**   Finesse your way up low-angle friction slab. Variations include or exclude nearby corners. Don't slip! 18 feet. FA: Robert Palais.

36   **(V0– R)**   Climb right side of narrow, left-leaning slab and escape right near the top. 18 feet. FA: Jeff Achey.

37   **Trapeze (V0 R)**   Swing up left side of arête at right end of steep, concave face. At top, make exposed, exciting traverse left along lip of boulder to easy step-off on left side. 18 feet. FA: Jeff Achey.

38   **Close Shave (V2 X)** ★   Climb very center of slightly concave, steep face to top. Razor-thin start and finish. Right-hand corner is not used at all while left-hand corner is used only for feet when approaching top. Pull over top at very highest point on face. To anchor TR, lasso pinnacle with long runner. 16 feet. FA: Henry Barber.

39   **Granite Enema (V0)** ★   To left of Close Shave start, hang from low big bucket, then move up and right to thin face holds. Continue to top using holds on face and left-hand corner. Fall and thou shalt receive a violent granite enema. 15 feet.

40   **Ain't No Tooth Up Here (V0)**   Climb up and out of awkward dihedral. 12 feet.

CRADLE ROCK

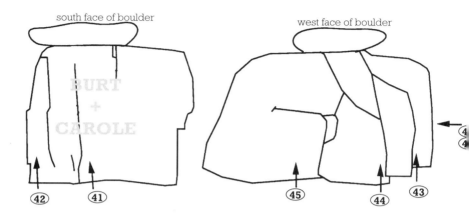

CRADLE ROCK (V0–V5)

Large boulder with smaller boulder cradled on top.

41   **Burt and Carole (V1– R)** ★   Climb committing crack through the lovers' graffiti. Can be done by laybacking crack or climbing thin face to left. If you don't feel comfortable on initial moves, use a TR. 17 feet. FA: Doug Gray.

42   **Cornercopia (V0–)**   Up outside corner. 17 feet.

43   **(V0–)**   Climb right-facing column that juts out from boulder. Use holds only on column. 16 feet.

44   **(V0–)**   Up huge vertical flake to top. 15 feet.

45   **Rockabye Baby (V0)** ★   Climb good flakes up steep face to left side of roof formed by smaller boulder cradled on top. 14 feet. FA: Doug Gray. Harder, exciting variation pulls directly over roof (FA: Mark Sonenfeld).

Smaller boulder 30 feet south of the Cradle Rock boulder offers three problems on the side opposite Cradle Rock.

46   **Riding The Pig (V0–)**   Hand traverse lip of boulder from right end to left end. 18 feet.

47   **Fusion Boots (V6)**   Steep face on right side of boulder. The right-hand arête is off-route. Most people who attempt this will feel like their boots are fused to the ground! 18 feet.

48   **Slapping The Pig's Genitals (V1)** ★★   Crouch down on left side of boulder, grab jugs on low shelf, raise feet off ground, hand

traverse right up ramp, shoot for lip of boulder on right side of overhanging dihedral and hand traverse along lip of boulder to right end. Got all that? Seriously, this is a great problem, but there are some further rules. If your feet even brush the ground after you begin, start over.

SMALLER CRADLE ROCK BOULDER

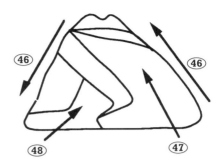

At the top of the overhanging dihedral is a big pointy hold. This hold is off-route as is the lip of the boulder left of the hold, but the lip of the boulder right of the pointy hold is fair game. All of the big footholds at the bottom of the overhanging dihedral are off-route as well. Not as contrived as it sounds. 10 feet.

JOHN ANDERSON ON CRADLE ROCK BOULDER.

BITCH BOULDER

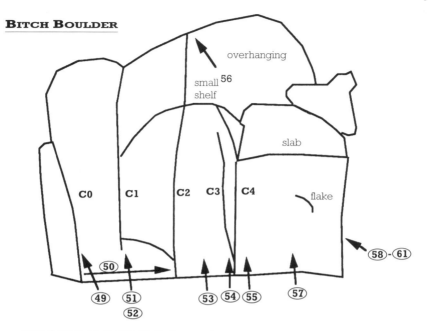

BITCH BOULDER (V0–V4)

The steepest and most impressive boulder in the area.

49 **Noisome Crack (V0–)**   Start at base of crack labeled C1. Reach up left for crack labeled C0 and climb this to top. 11 feet.

50 **Bitch Traverse (V2/V3)** ★★   Perform low traverse across front of boulder starting at crack labeled C0 and ending at arête on right end. V3 if you continue traverse, staying low, to right side of arête. 20 feet.

51 **Repetition (V1+)** ★★ **TR**   Climb steep crack labeled C1 to top. Crack C0 is off-route. Best problem in area (worth repeating). Toprope is required. 16 feet. FFA: Doug Gray.

52 **Inverse Traverse (V0+)**   Start up Repetition, hand traverse right along right-arching seam and gain small shelf. Escape to right. 14 feet. FA: Doug Gray.

53 **Pinnacle (V2)**   Climb cracks labeled C2 and C3, and any holds in between, up to small shelf. Escape to right. For easier variation, use corner above crack C4 (V1). Height sensitive. It is said that a legendary lord of the boulders (J.S.) caught his foot in the crack, fell on his head, forgot his name, forgot where his car was, forgot what he was doing there…. 12 feet. FA: Doug Gray.

BITCH BOULDER

54   **Life Is A Bitch (V2)** ★   Climb cracks labeled C3 and C4 with right foot in C4. Exit up and right onto slab. An important edge left of C3 is on-route for left foot. 10 feet.

55   **Crucifixion (V0)** ★   Climb crack labeled C4 with body on right side. Exit up onto slab. The "official" way to do this is with left foot in C4 and right foot smeared on face, but who cares. FA: Doug Gray 10 feet.

56   **Playing House (with a Roof) (V0– X)**   Variation finish. From the slab, step up left on small shelf and climb overhang to top. Normally done with TR. FA: Doug Gray

57   **Static Cling (V2)** ★   Pull on obvious flake to gain slopers at bottom of slab (like trying to grab a beach ball with one hand). Finish with tenuous mantle onto slab (use spotter!). Stay away from C4 and corner above C4. Easier variation starts further right and climbs left side of arête. 12 feet. FA: Doug Gray.

The next three problems are on the right side of the Bitch Boulder.

58   **Shin-up (V2 R)** ★   Begin standing on rock embedded in ground below right side of arête, just around corner from Static Cling. Climb right side of arête and follow difficult layback seam to top. The right-arching seam to right, which belongs to Chainstitch, is completely off-route. TR recommended. 14 feet. FA: Doug Gray.

59 **Chain Stitch (V4 R)** ★   Start a few feet right of Shin-up and climb desperate, right-arching seam to top. Height dependent. TR required. Originally done as an aid problem, hence the name "Pull one stitch and they'll all go!" 14 feet. FA: Doug Gray, Robert Palais, Pete Worthington (on aid, A4).

60 **The Stand (Project) (V??)**   Start at a conspicuous, chest-level jug on otherwise blank face, 5 feet right of Chain Stitch. A few thin edges might make it possible to stand up on the jug. Before this is worked, a crucial layback micro-edge should be reinforced (flexes when pulled) or this will forever remain a project. 14 feet.

61 **Quick Access (V0–)**   Easy crack left of gully between Bitch Boulder and adjacent boulder. At top of crack, move up and right to top. 14 feet.

62 **Bulbous (V0)**   Smaller boulder perched above gully behind Bitch Boulder forms bulging overhang. Slap and grope your way over this. 12 feet.

ED'S SECRET SLAB (V0–V3)

This boulder features an excellent slab problem with minuscule granulations for holds (V3 ★★). First ascent by Ed Van Steenwyk. Well worth the 10-minute hike if you know where it is. If we told you, the boulder's name would have to be changed….

CHAPTER 2

HUNTERDON COUNTY

SOURLAND MOUNTAIN RESERVATION
Near Hopewell
Granite boulders; 13 problems V0-V4; Local interest

A wooded nature preserve strewn with countless granite boulders similar to those found at Cradle Rock, 6 miles away. Unfortunately only a small number are climbable, but these are quiet and secluded.

ACCESS ISSUES   The authors are not aware of any explicit access policy although this does not guarantee that such policy does not exist. You must take full responsibility for your own actions. This guidebook describes potential climbing resources but does not imply in any way that you have permission to use those resources for climbing or any other purpose. You alone are responsible for determining whether any form of recreational activity is permitted. If climbing is not permitted, the recommended response is to comply fully, but at the same time, to form an activist organization to lobby for open access.

DIRECTIONS (FROM DOWNTOWN HOPEWELL)   From East Broad Street (Rt 518) in downtown Hopewell, turn onto Greenwood Avenue North—which becomes Hopewell-Wertsville Rd/Rt 607—and drive 2.6 miles (passing Mignella's at 2.1) to reach the Sourland Mountain Reservation entrance on your right. About 100 feet from the entrance is an obvious pulloff where you can park.

From the pulloff, walk along the woods road for about 20 minutes. When your legs inform you that you are walking uphill, become alert. When the woods road takes a sharp 90-degree turn to the left, stop. A small trail leads to the right and another small trail with white markers continues straight ahead. Follow the white marked trail straight ahead for several hundred feet (about 2.5 minutes) until you come to a chain-sawed tree stump on the left (the resulting log lies across the trail). You may also see the remains of a tree fort here. At this point, walk left off the trail and into the woods for about 100 feet and you will discover two boulders obviously suitable for bouldering. Many smaller and less interesting boulders are nearby.

We have heard but not verified that easier access is possible by parking near a ball field and approaching the boulders from the east via a hiking trail which parallels the 3M Road.

SOURLAND MOUNTAIN PRESERVE

1   **(V1)**   Thin face. The good flakes on Problem 2 are off-route.

2   **(V0–)**   Outside corner with good flakes.

3   **(V2)**   Holds on Problem 2 and crack to right are off-route (contrived). Thin top-out.

4   **(V0–)**   Easy crack.

5   **(V0–)**   Easy crack.

6   **(V0)**   On rounded pinnacle-like boulder, climb up several feet right of corner.

7   **The Egg (V4)** ★   Start beneath blank, overhanging bulge resembling surface of monstrous egg. Leap for holds (height dependent) and fire for top.

8   **Flakeout (V1)** ★   Start around corner from The Egg below cluster of flakes on steep face. Climb straight up to boulder's high-point while avoiding slab to right.

9   **(V0+)**   On main boulder, climb face three feet right of corner/cleft (which is off-route).

10   **(V0+)**   Face 4 feet left of obvious crack.

11   **(V0+)**   Face 2 feet left of obvious crack (which is off-route).

SOURLAND MOUNTAIN RESERVATION

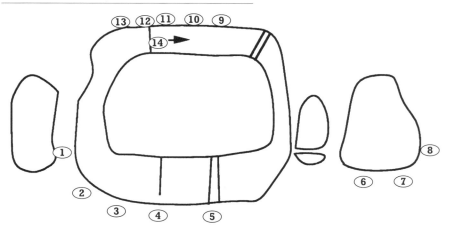

12   (V0–)   Obvious crack.

13   (V0–)   Face 2 feet right of obvious crack (which is off-route).

14   **Sourland Traverse (V2)** ★   Step up at crack and traverse left until standing in corner/cleft. A few laps on this will light your wrists on fire.

BUZZARD'S BUTTE

South of Frenchtown
20'-25' shale cliffs; Routes 5.1 to 5.10d, leading; Local interest

A small shale cliff in a semi-secluded wooded area overlooking a multi-tiered but modest waterfall. The area is located just off of Rt 29, south of Frenchtown and north of Stockton. The shale is good quality Lockatong Argillite, similar to that at Ralph Stover State Park, but improved by the lack of the notoriously friable Brunswick Shale. The climbing is mostly on vertical faces and cracks. The routes are generally top-roped although there is a nice fingercrack which makes a worthwhile lead with decent protection.

ACCESS ISSUES   The authors are not aware of any explicit access policy although this does not guarantee that such policy does not exist. You must take full responsibility for your own actions. This guidebook describes potential climbing resources but does not imply in any way that you have permission to use those resources for climbing or any other purpose. You alone are responsible for determining whether any form of recreational activity is permitted. If climbing is not permitted, the recommended response is to comply fully, but at the same time, to form an activist organization to lobby for open access.

DIRECTIONS: From Bridge St. (the main business street) in Frenchtown, turn south onto Trenton Ave/Rt 29 and travel 6.1 miles south to a pulloff on the left side of the road. Alternatively, travel north on Rt 29 from Stockton to reach the pulloff on the right side of the road (pulloff is 5.3 miles north of junction of Rt 29 and Rt 519). The pulloff is on the north end of a short guard rail which guards the stream and waterfall mentioned above. Park in the pulloff and hike 300 feet up a trail on the left side of the stream to reach the cliffs.

Note: There is room for only a few cars to park. If the pulloff has no room for your vehicle, the cliff has no room for your party!

All routes are 20 to 25 feet high.

1   (V2)   Obvious thin-face boulder problem on outcrop uphill and left of main cliff. Height dependent.

2   (1)   Easy crack. Beware of loose and hollow rock.

3   (12a)   Climb very thin face between two crack systems. The cracks and good holds immediately next to them are off-route. Contrived route for those seeking difficulty.

BUZZARD'S BUTTE

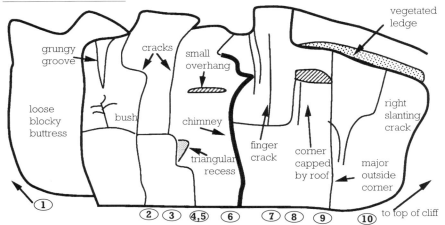

4   **(6)**   Climb up to a triangular recess, step left and continue up crack to top.

5   **(10c)**   Climb up to triangular recess. Traverse somewhat right, pull over small overhang, and continue to top.

6   **(10d/11a)**   Start 4 feet left of chimney. Staying away from chimney, climb up and left past small overhang to top.

7   **Cracker Jack (7/7+ G/PG) ★**   Climb nice fingercrack which starts about 10 feet above ground. At top of crack, either continue up face pulling over top at highest point (5.7+) or bail off left a bit below highest point.

8   **Ring Ding Roof (10d) ★**   Start below and a few feet left of corner capped by roof. Climb up and right into corner, pass roof on left side, and make crux moves straight up to ledge.

9   **(8+)**   Start below and a few feet right of corner capped by roof. Climb up and left into corner and pass around roof on right side.

10   **Yard and Ballocks (9+)**   Grunt and heave up awkward right-slanting crack to vegetated ledge.

REIGELSVILLE CLIFFS

Near Reigelsville
180' moderate route above Delaware River; Dirty & vegetated; Local interest

There are numerous scattered cliffs and outcrops on both sides of the Delaware River near Reigelsville. A few hardcore adventurers have braved the loose, poor quality rock to establish routes on these cliffs.

On the New Jersey side at least one route has reportedly been done on a set of tiered slabs and faces which together afford about 180 feet of climbing and scrambling. Those who persevere to the top are rewarded with a great view of the river. The rock is similar to that at the Delaware Water Gap but is of even lesser quality. Much of the climbing is Class 4 or 5.0 but there are a few harder sections which can be climbed or avoided as you see fit. The route is seasonal: except for the late fall and winter months, the cliff is completely covered with poison ivy! A description of this route is given below.

On the Pennsylvania side there are cliffs up to 300 feet high, known by many as the "Kintersville Cliffs" or the "Delaware Palisades." The multi-pitch ice climbing here has attracted climbers from as far as New England. Although the rock quality is very poor, a handful of rock routes have reportedly been established.

ACCESS ISSUES   The authors are not aware of any explicit access policy although this does not guarantee that such policy does not exist. You must take full responsibility for your own actions. This guidebook describes potential climbing resources but does not imply in any way that you have permission to use those resources for climbing or any other purpose. You alone are responsible for determining whether any form of recreational activity is permitted. If climbing is not permitted, the recommended response is to comply fully, but at the same time, to form an activist organization to lobby for open access.

DIRECTIONS   For the NJ Cliffs, approach the Reigelsville Bridge from the NJ side as if you were going to cross the Delaware River, but veer right onto River Rd just before the bridge (not shown on some street maps). Follow River Rd north for 1.0 mile to a pulloff on the right, across the street from train tracks. Walk another 50 feet north along the road and then scramble up to the base of the lower tier.

For the Kintersville Cliffs, cross the Reigelsville Bridge into PA, turn left onto Rt 611S, drive south a few miles, then turn left onto Rt 32S. The cliffs loom high above the west side of Rt 32.

1   (??)   One-hundred-and-eighty-foot route on NJ side. Scramble up to base of steep slab and follow conspicuous thin crack to ledge. Scramble up and left to roof split by off-width crack and climb this to large ledges. Continue up easy slabs to top. Technical difficulty and protection unknown. Wire-brush could be most important item on rack.

Nearby areas: *About a third of a mile south of the Reigelsville Bridge, on the east side of River Road is reportedly a small outcrop. Warning: We do not know if this is on public property.*

MUSCONETCONG GORGE NATURE PRESERVE

Near Riegelsville
Granite outcrops up to 25 feet; Routes 5.3 to 5.12a, leading; Bouldering V0-V3

Five granite outcrops line a wooded hillside overlooking the Musconetcong River in a secluded location reached after 20 minutes of hiking. Clean, solid granite faces, slabs and cracks with a wide range of difficulty. Other boulders and outcrops can be found scattered in the surrounding woods.

ACCESS ISSUES   The authors are not aware of any explicit access policy although this does not guarantee that such policy does not exist. You must take full responsibility for your own actions. This guidebook describes potential climbing resources but does not imply in any way that you have permission to use those resources for climbing or any other purpose. You alone are responsible for determining whether any form of recreational activity is permitted. If climbing is not permitted, the recommended response is to comply fully, but at the same time, to form an activist organization to lobby for open access.

DIRECTIONS   From Rt 78W, take Exit 7 and turn right onto Rt 173W (from Rt 78E, take Exit 6 instead). Follow Rt 173W for 1.2 miles and turn left onto Rt 639W. Follow this 2.8 miles to a stop sign, then turn left onto Rt 519S. Follow 519S through a left turn and then past a large paper mill plant on the left. The plant will serve as a landmark when you are hiking to the outcrops

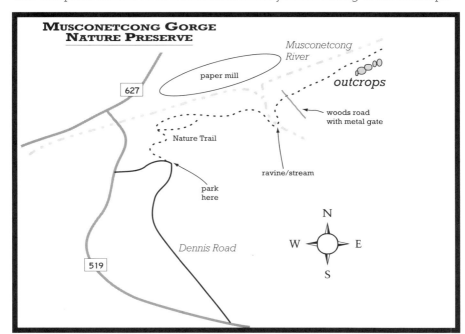

MUSCONETCONG GORGE NATURE PRESERVE

which are on the second hillside beyond the plant. Drive part way up a steep hill and turn left onto Dennis Rd (a dirt road). Follow Dennis Rd for 0.2 mile and park at a pulloff on the left in front of a sign for the "Musconetcong Nature Preserve."

Expect twenty minutes of hiking to the outcrops. From the pulloff, follow the nature trail into the woods and down a hill. Zigzag a few times, then turn sharply right onto another trail segment which runs along the hillside. As you walk the trail, you should be able to see the paper mill below on the left, foliage allowing. Soon the trail follows the right side of a ravine and descends to a stream. After crossing the stream, the trail, now quite indistinct, turns left and follows the opposite bank in the direction of the paper mill. Soon, the trail crosses a woods road with a metal gate on the left. Continue ahead on the trail for a fifth of a mile. The outcrops are off the right side of the trail, about 200 feet up on the hillside.

When the trees have their foliage, the outcrops may not be visible from the trail. You should leave the trail just as it converges with a dirt road, with the Musconetcong River just beyond. At the point where you leave the trail, the dirt road is about 40 feet to the left of the trail.

HAZARDS   Although the rock is solid, there may be some loose holds. Hunting is legal in the area with a permit, so make sure you cannot be mistaken for a deer.

OUTCROP 1

Leftmost of five outcrops.

1   (??)   The steep face on east side of outcrop looks enticing but should be avoided because of a sharp, heavy flake that is about to fall off.

2   (??)   Hard problem starts at overhang just left of small tree next to outcrop.

3   (??)   Desperate arête just right of small tree next to outcrop.

4   (V0–)   Easy crack on front side of outcrop.

OUTCROP 2

Distinguished by a steep slab, which is fairly blank except for a vertical seam.

5   (V0)   Up on east side of outcrop, start at thinnest part of face, climb past several shelves and top out at highest point.

6   **Balance of Power (11d?)** ★   Climb difficult vertical seam up steep slab. It may be necessary to wire-brush moss out of the seam. FA: Mike Flood (lead with gear pre-placed), Spring 1993.

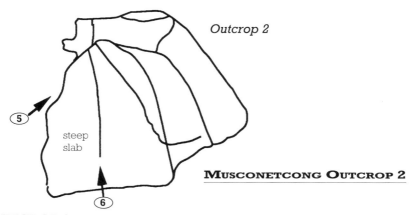

Outcrop 2

steep
slab

MUSCONETCONG OUTCROP 2

OUTCROP 3

One of the two largest outcrops, separated from Outcrop 4 by 20 feet.

5   **(V0–)**   Uphill on left side of outcrop, climb short face with tiered shelves.

6   **(V0+)**   On left side of outcrop, climb up just left of tree avoiding any big holds and laybacks on left. Awkward, tricky problem.

7   **(V2 X)**   Arête at left end of outcrop. The crux is tenuous, so use TR.

8   **(2)**   Toprope. The corners of the chimney form two arêtes. Climb left side of left arête.

9   **(9)** ★   Toprope. Thin cracks on right side of right arête formed by chimney. To get started, step over from right.

10   **(5– G)** ★   Obvious fingercrack.

11   **(3)**   Toprope right side of arête at right end of outcrop. Easy.

OUTCROP 4

Twenty feet from Outcrop 3.

12   **(10c G)** ★   Steep crack at left end of outcrop. Short but interesting lead climb.

13   **Terminator (12a)** ★   Toprope. Climb thin face just right of crack without touching crack. Tricky start. Fingery and reachy. FTR: Mike Flood, Spring 1993.

14   **(11d??)**   Toprope. The direct start to the steep arête is extreme and probably has not been done. Instead, do the initial moves on Terminator, traverse right to buckets part-way up the arête and continue to the top.

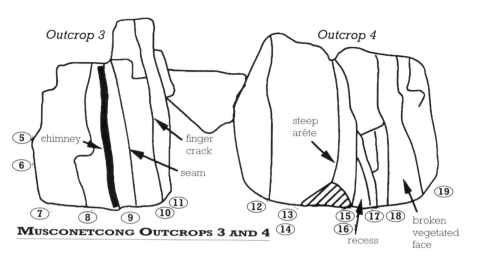

MUSCONETCONG OUTCROPS 3 AND 4

15   (12b??)   Toprope. Use overhanging seam on right side of steep
arête to get started on arête which is then climbed to top.

16   (A5)   Overhanging seam in alcove looks like challenging aid
problem.

17   (V0–)   Climb fingercrack in back of alcove (without stemming
alcove) until you can escape right.

18   (V0–)   Short, conspicuous fist crack that starts 7 feet above
ground.

19   (V0)   On far right end of outcrop, climb smooth face with several
slight dihedrals.

OUTCROP 5

The smallest and rightmost outcrop has a few boulder problems.

20   (V2)   Short face immediately left of corner/crack. Don't use
corner/crack or large holds near left end of short face. Height
dependent.

21   (V0–)   Stem up corner/crack.

22   (V0+) ★   Exciting narrow face on right side of corner/crack. The
jug on right side of start is off-route.

23   (V3??)   Steep face with left-slanting seam uphill from
corner/crack.

TEETERTOWN NATURE PRESERVE
Near Califon
Granite boulders; 23 problems V0-V4; Small but worthwhile area

Small bouldering area overlooking a ravine in a wooded nature preserve. There are a handful of climbable boulders but these are excellent. Many of the problems are on slabs of varying steepness with nubbins and small edges for holds.

ACCESS ISSUES   In the past, bouldering has generally been tolerated while roped climbing has been forbidden. This fragile acceptance will end as soon as any "incident" occurs. Discretion, minimal impact, and safe, responsible conduct are absolutely critical. At all times keep in mind that this is a private nature preserve. Vehicles bearing visitors to the preserve frequently pass just below the boulders. Do not bring any climbing equipment or attempt to set up ropes. Anything beyond safe scrambling and bouldering will jeopardize access.

The authors are not aware of any explicit access policy although this does not guarantee that such policy does not exist. You must take full responsibility for your own actions. This guidebook describes potential climbing resources but does not imply in any way that you have permission to use those resources for climbing or any other purpose. You alone are responsible for determining whether any form of recreational activity is permitted. If climbing is not permitted, the recommended response is to comply fully, but at the same time, to form an activist organization to lobby for open access.

DIRECTIONS   From Rt 31, about 1.9 miles north of Rt 78, turn east onto Rt 513 (just north of Mountain Sports climbing shop). Drive 6.5 miles to town of Califon and turn left onto Sliker Rd (just past A&P Supermarket on left). Drive 0.8 mile and turn right onto Teetertown Rd. Drive about 1.0 mile (stay left at fork) and then turn left onto Hollow Brook Rd. Continue straight and enter the preserve via a dirt road. The boulders are above the left side of the road about 0.1 mile past the stone bridge which spans the ravine.

Important   Do not obstruct traffic when parking along the narrow dirt road. In

PN ON BOULDER PROBLEM AT TEETERTOWN NATURAL PRESERVE. PHOTO: RUTHANNE WAGNER.

particular, do not park in pulloffs next to the one-lane bridges because these allow cars traveling in opposite directions to pass each other. This leaves parking room for only one or two vehicles but there are only four boulders anyway.

Further down on the right side of the dirt road is a 20-foot cliff. Do not climb here because the rock is loose, dirty, and would require the use of a rope.

Hazards   Some of the problems are thin and tenuous. Scope out the landings before you attempt a problem and always use an alert and competent spotter.

The diagram shows the boulders as seen from the dirt road.

1   **(V0–)**   Romp up easy slab starting at flake. Don't blow the start. 15 feet.

2   **(V0–)**   Hand traverse up left-rising arête. 14 feet.

3   **(V0+)**   Between boulders, start directly beneath highest point on right-hand boulder and climb up to it without touching left-rising seam. For easier variation (V0), start a few feet further right and angle up and left to highest point without using left-rising seam. 12 feet.

4   **(V0)**   Start between boulders and climb left-hand boulder. 10 feet.

5   **(V2)**   Climb arête without using zigzagging seam on right side of arête. 11 feet.

6   **(V0+)** ★   The crack. Don't use flake belonging to next problem. 12 feet.

7   **(V0)** ★   Climb slab on left side of crack using obvious flake-hold. 11 feet.

8   **(V2)** ★   Climb blank slab between arête and obvious flake-hold without using either. This will test your thin slab technique. 11 feet.

9   **(V0–)**   Arête. 11 feet.

10   **(V??) Project**   Traverse from left to right behind boulder. Top of boulder and holds 6 inches below top are off-route as are detached rocks at base. Start with your left hand on left edge of boulder and traverse right to touch big log leaning against boulder. Nasty, awkward problem for little people. 18 feet.

11   **(V0–)** ★   Climb slab near right end of boulder using obvious flake. 12 feet.

12   **(V1)** ★   Center of slab. 14 feet.

13   **(V0)**   Slab near left end of boulder. 15 feet.

14   **(V1)**   Start at left end of boulder and perform low traverse to right end. 16 feet.

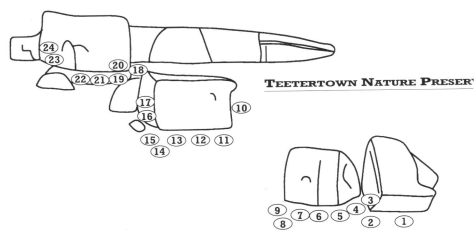

TEETERTOWN NATURE PRESER'

15 **(V0)**   Left side of arête. 12 feet.

16 **(V4)**   Climb center of steep thin face to gain obvious flake-like jug. The further left you start, the easier it is, but the official problem begins with "push-off" foot touching platform-like rock embedded in ground. Place push-off foot on ground so that it touches part of platform-like rock that is closest to problem. 12 feet.

17 **(V0)**   Slap your way up rounded arête. 11 feet.

18 **(V0–)**   The right side of arête. 13 feet.

The next four problems would require a toprope to be climbed safely, so should not be attempted at the present time.

19 **(V0 R)**   The left side of arête. Ledge above and to right of start is off-route. See warning above. 16 feet.

20 **(V0+ R)**   Same as previous problem but don't touch arête. See warning above. 16 feet.

21 **Pop Goes The Nubbin (V3 R/X)**   Center of steep thin face. This tough nubbin-haul would get at least one star if it was safe. Unfortunately the friable nubbins can't be trusted and the landing is bad. See warning above. 16 feet.

22 **(V0+ R)**   Left side of steep face. Left-facing corner with easy layback at left edge of face is off-route. Thin near top with ghastly landing below. See warning above. 16 feet.

23 **(V2–)**   Steep face just left of ramp-like corner. Big jugs on left and ramp-like corner on right are off-route. 11 feet.

24 **(V1)** ★   Start at far left end of boulder and perform low traverse right to rest position on outside corner. Stop here or continue right following path of least resistance across nubbin face to right end of boulder (feet are about 2 feet above overhang, scary). 30 feet.

CHAPTER 3

WARREN COUNTY

JENNY JUMP STATE FOREST
Near Hope
25- to 35-foot granite cliffs; Short TR routes, 5.1 to 5.12-; Local interest

Forested area with 25- to 35-foot granite cliffs. Sections of grungy rock are interspersed with suprisingly clean, steep granite faces. The climbs tend to be either easy or bouldery and difficult. A cave-like overhang on an outcrop near the park entrance also has potential.

ACCESS ISSUES   A special-use permit is presently required to climb in NJ state parks. We are told that in the past such permits have been issued only to commercial guiding services. However, in 1996 the NJ state park administrative code will come under review. This presents an excellent opportunity to make the code more favorable to individual climbers (who after all vote and pay taxes just like other recreational users!). Since this opportunity will not come again this century, we recommend writing a letter to your local politicians (freeholders, congresspersons, senators) and to the Director of NJ State Park Services, CN404, Trenton, NJ 08625, urging that climbing be recognized as a legitimate use of state parks.

HISTORY   A first descent occurred here back in colonial days. A father and his daughter were picking berries in the woods when they were discovered by a band of Indians. The father, fearing that his daughter would be abducted by the Indians, urged her to cast herself from a precipice and thereby preserve her honor. "Jenny, jump!" he shouted— and so she did. The Indians, no doubt, were astonished. If you climb here, you could be reversing her historic descent!

DIRECTIONS   From Rt 80, take Exit 12 for Hope and turn onto Rt 521S. Continue for 1 mile into Hope and turn left onto Rt 519N (Hope-Johnsonburg Rd). Following signs for Jenny Jump State Forest, continue for 1.1 miles and turn right onto Shiloh Rd. Drive 1.1 miles and turn right onto State Park Rd. Proceed 1 mile and turn left into the park's main entrance. For the granite cliffs, follow signs to campsites #15-21. Park near the restrooms (between campsites 19 and 20) and use the map below to find the cliffs. To get to the cave boulder (of lesser interest) from the park entrance, stay right at several forks and park in the main parking lot near the restrooms. The cave boulder is on the hillside overlooking the white office buildings (see map).

All difficulty ratings are estimated—until we climb here on a dry day!

1   **Cave Boulder (V??)**   A few problems will go up after cleaning.

2   **Pyramid Boulder (V0-??)**   Striking 25-foot boulder rises above lesser boulders in talus field. Resembles pyramid when viewed from direction of swamp.

3   **(1??)**   Easy crack just right of blank face.

4   **(7??)**   Small seam 5 feet left of chimney.

5   **(10??)**   On right side of chimney is steep, bouldery start followed by easy low-angle climbing.

6   **(2??)**   Follow easiest line up 35-foot buttress.

7   **(11??)**   Short, narrow, overhanging face which faces left. Harder if obvious jug on right is not used.

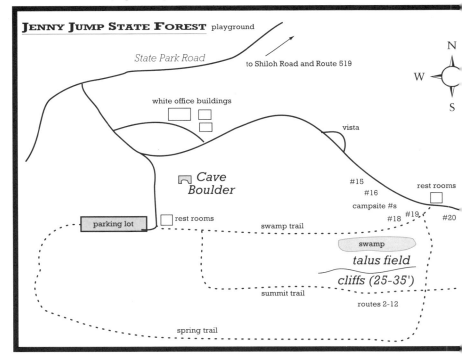

JENNY JUMP: MAIN CLIFFS

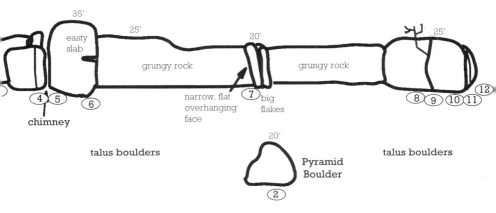

8   **(11??)**   Pair of tiny seams just left of crack with small tree growing from it.

9   **(10??)**   Crack with tree growing from it (might take protection if cleaned out).

10   **(12–??)**   Follow thin seam up steep face just right of crack with tree growing from it. Very thin!

11   **(10??)**   Left side of arête.

12   **(2??)**   Easy crack on right-facing lesser-angle rock. around corner right of the previous route.

DELAWARE WATER GAP
(MT. TAMMANY & MT. MINSI)

140- to 280-foot metaquartzite cliffs; 205 trad routes, 5.0 to 5.11, 1-3 pitches

A Climbing Guide to the Delaware Water Gap by Michael Steele is the best source of information on routes at The Gap. This chapter merely supplements Steele's guide by providing a recommended route list from the perspective of the authors. One criticism that has sometimes been made of Steele's guide is that it does not tell you how to locate the climbs on the NJ side. We have tried to remedy that.

There are two major crags at The Gap, Mt Tammany on the NJ side and Mt Minsi on the PA side. Both crags are in the Delaware Water Gap National Recreational Area. Mt Tammany has the largest and tallest cliffs in NJ, reaching heights of over 200 feet. The crags are part of the same Silurian formation as the Shawangunks and are composed of the same type of metaquartzite rock, although the rock quality is generally inferior to that at the Shawangunks.

Each crag offers about 100 established routes reaching 5.11 in difficulty. Most are two pitch routes and almost all have traditional protection. At present there are only a handful of bolts at The Gap, all on the PA side. Many of the routes could use a good cleaning since they see little traffic, although this is less of a problem on the classic lines. Many of the climbs have an adventurous feel because of the combination of vertiginous exposure, vegetated or loose rock and a general lack of the usual signs of climbing activity (no pitons, bolts, slings, or chalk). Most of the routes have good protection at crux sections, although there may be longish, sometimes scary runouts on easier sections.

ACCESS ISSUES   Climbing at the Delaware Water Gap is an accepted activity well known to the park. At one time, the park required climbers to fill out a card at the visitor's center before and after each visit. Registration is now optional, although still recommended. In contrast to NJ state parks, a permit is required only for commercial guiding.

DIRECTIONS   To Mt Tammany—Heading west on Rt 80, you pass right under the main climbing wall (which faces south) as you drive through The Gap. Park in the first rest area on the right, about 0.25 mile after passing through The Gap. This is also the parking area for the Red Dot Trail, a recommended hike to the top of Mt. Tammany. If you wish to stop by the

MT. TAMMANY ON THE NEW JERSEY SIDE OF DELAWARE WATER GAP. PHOTO: LYLE LANG

visitor's center (where you can register), drive down a short road next to the parking lot, turn left, cross under Rt 80 and turn right.

From the rest area, walk back along or behind the retaining wall bordering Rt 80 to reach the base of the climbing wall. This can be done without ever setting foot on the pavement of Rt 80. DO NOT WALK ALONG RT 80 ITSELF! You will be blown over and squashed like an armadillo by the endless stream of trucks. To avoid walking in the road, begin on the grass verge, then follow a trail that stays behind the retaining wall or the concrete divider all the way to the bend in the road. Just around the bend is a step trail that leads up to the base of the first climb, Dead Man's Curve. Keep the name of this route in mind at all times on the approach to the cliff, and stay off the road.

HAZARDS   Do not trust any fixed pitons. They will fail.

Even if you are normally too stylish to wear a helmet, consider donning one at The Gap because the routes are somewhat alpine in nature. If the belayer will be in an exposed position beneath the leader, the belayer should definitely wear a helmet.

Ticks and wasps.

Poison ivy, identifiable by clusters of three waxy or shiny leaves.

Communication between the leader and belayer is often difficult, especially when climbing near Rt 80 on the NJ side. This is exacerbated by the winding nature of the routes which often leaves the leader and belayer out of sight and earshot of each other. A useful technique is for the leader to always put the second on belay before taking up the rope. This way, the second knows that when all the rope is taken up, it is safe to climb.

RECOMMENDED ROUTES   For Mt. Tammany: The Rib (5.3 PG), Triumvirate (5.4 PG), Sobriety Test (5.7 PG), Double Overhang (5.8 G), Corkscrew (5.8 PG), Death Don't Have No Mercy (5.9-/9+ PG), Tree Toad Fracture (5.9 G), Say Your Pwayers Wabbit (5.9+ PG), Ride Of The Valkyries (5.10b PG), Chinese Handcuffs (5.11a TR).

For Mt Minsi: Surprise (5.4 G/PG), Heroine Hypnosis (5.5- G), Hell and High Water (5.5 PG), High Falls (5.8+ G/PG), Chieftain (5.8+ PG), Point of No Return (5.9- PG), Bird Dog (5.10a G/PG), Raptor of the Steep (5.10a PG), Gap View Heights (5.10c G/PG), Voyage of the Damned (5.10c PG), Razor's Edge (5.11a G/PG), Morning Sickness (5.11 PG).

The following comparisons should help you decide whether to visit Mt Tammany (New Jersey) or Mt Minsi (Pennsylvania).

• More sunshine (less shade): Mt Tammany

• Higher quality rock: Mt Minsi

- Cleaner routes: Mt Tammany

- Easier approach: Mt Tammany

- Quieter atmosphere: Mt Minsi

- Toproping/short routes: Mt Tammany

- Quality and quantity of 5.8 to 5.9 routes: Mt Tammany

- Quality and quantity of 5.10 to 5.11 routes: Mt Minsi

Below is a selected route list.. The reader should reference Michael Steele's guidebook for complete route information. The log book at the visitor's center has corrections and additions to Steele's guide.

Mt Tammany (NJ side): The descriptions start at the top of the trail up from Rt 80, and proceed from left to right. Only the best routes are described here. For a complete listing see Steele's guide.

1   **Dead Man's Curve (8+ G/PG)** ★   A short route which starts almost in the west-bound lane of Rt 80. Actual start is at head of trail up from Rt 80, below conspicuous right-arching crack. Climb crack, traverse right to a block, and climb this to a belay.

2   **JG (or The Chiseler) (4 G/PG)** ★   About 90 feet up the trail from Dead Man's Curve is a small square chimney with the initials JG carved at the bottom. Climb chimney and wall above, finishing left of overhang.

3   **Premature Exasperation (11a PG/R)** ★   To right of JG, climb up to a small overhang 15 feet above ground, pull the hang slightly right of center onto a very thin and technical slab and move up to a horizontal at 30 feet (a little run out). Exit by moving left to JG. Well named! FA: Michael Steele and Henry McMahon, late 1980s.

Forty feet to the right of JG is a big, blocky, left-facing corner that forms the left end of a protruding buttress. The front of the buttress has a small overhang just above the ground with a small tree growing right next to it. The next three routes, which climb the front of this buttress, can be easily top-roped by walking further up the trail and scrambling back left along ledges. Use long slings from a tree.

4   **Chinese Handcuffs (11a)** ★   Top rope. Excellent small overhang and technical face at left end of protruding buttress.

5   **Little Shop of Horrors (8+ G)**   Climb thin crack through center of low overhang behind small tree, then up the face above to the ledge. The second pitch, which continues above the ledge, is probably not worth doing. FA: Michael Steele and Todd Swain, late 1980s.

6   **Mr Cohesive (9)** ★   Toprope. Overhang and face between Little Shop and outside corner.

As you are hiking up the trail from the previous routes, scan the bottom part of the cliff for a steep, thin, bulging face which eases off after 25 feet to loose-looking ledges and horizontals. This face (Die Hard) begins from a ledge just above the trail and commands attention for its relatively high quality and apparent difficulty. Higher up on the cliff is a prominent protruding nose. There is also a hemlock, the first encountered, growing out of the talus slope about 100 feet from the cliff.

7   **Die Hard (10d)** ★   Top rope. The steep, thin, bulging face. To reach the horizontals used for toprope anchors, lead up the left-facing corner at the right edge of the bulging face until you can traverse left above it. FTR: Michael Steele and Jeff Chiniewiz, late 1980s.

8   **Say Your Pwayers Wabbit (9+ PG)** ★★   Begins 40 feet right of Die Hard and surmounts the wild-looking overhangs near the top of the cliff. The following variation avoids awkward and unpleasant belays. P1: Climb up and belay on spacious ledge below the chimney of Chimney Sweep, the next climb to the right. P2: Using long runners, traverse left and continue through the crux sections as described in Steele's guidebook. FA: Michael Steele and Nick Miskowsi, late 1980s.

Some 40 to 50 feet right of Wabbit, look for a tree high on the cliff with rappel slings around it. Just below this tree, the conspicuous Trapdoor Chimney (5.5-, not described here) passes through a roof. The next two climbs pull the roof left of the chimney.

9   **The Hangman (7+ G)**   Thirty right of Wabbit, at an indentation, right of two large oaks. The first pitch is mostly a scramble to reach a belay below the crux hang. FA: Michael Steele and Nick Miskowsi, late 1980s.

10   **Well Hung (10d PG)** ★   A tough overhanging problem to test your virility. Same first pitch as The Hangman. Since the crux overhangs of both routes are right next to each other, one can climb up and down the The Hangman's crux as a warmup and simply leave in the protection for extra security.

About 80 feet right of the previous described tree with rappel slings is a recess (a huge chimney) known as the Class Four Ramp. Look for a tree 12 feet back from the cliff with orange paint at its base. If all else fails, the ramp can found by walking uphill 135 paces from JG.

11   **Class Four Ramp (1)** ★   Climb the left-hand inside corner of the huge chimney. For the competent climber this is the easiest descent route from the top of the cliff. An easy downclimb. It is also straightforward to set up a rappel here.

12   **Cheatstone (V0/V0+)** ★   About 30 feet right of Class Four Ramp
      is a low overhang six feet above the ground. The best boulder
      problems at Mt. Tammany are here. One problem climbs a steep
      face just left of the low overhang. While a cheatstone is often used
      to reach better starting holds, the problem can be done without it
      (harder but makes for safer landing). Many people will use a
      toprope. An easier, shorter problem turns the lip of the low
      overhang.

13   **Ride Of The Valkyries (10b PG)** ★★   Begins 45 feet right of
      Class Four Ramp, just right of Cheatstone's low overhang. The
      slightly overhanging crux wall is in an exciting, exposed position
      near the top of the cliff. FA: Michael Steele and Henry McMahon,
      late 1980s.

*The huge and ominous darker-colored wall facing the road, between Routes
38 and 46, is known as The Black Wall. To the right of this is the Triumvirate
Wall which contains the classic Gap route Triumvirate.*

*In the photo of this part of the cliff, the Class Four Ramp is at the extreme left,
and the dark section of cliff just left of center is the Black Wall. The
conspicuous arete between the dark wall and the main sunlit face is the aptly-
named Shadow Line (Route 44 in Steele's guide, although not one of our
selections). Triumvirate goes essentially straight up through center of picture,
whereas The Rib climbs the white face slightly to the right of the center.*

TRIUMVIRATE SECTION OF MT. TAMMANY CLIFF. PHOTO: LYLE LANGE.

14   **Triumvirate (4 PG) ★★★**   The start can be identified by a yellow circle with a cross inside it painted near the base of the route, on a 12-foot high slab, next to a tall oak tree. The route begins 8 feet to the right of the paint mark, up some steps between this slab and a large detached slab on the right. Looking up from the ground one can see three triangular roofs, the lowest pointing to the right and

THE START OF TRIUMVIRATE. THE ROUTE GOES UP THE CONSPICUOUS CHIMNEY IN THE VERY CENTER OF THE PHOTO AND HEADS UP RIGHT TO THE FIRST BELAY. PHOTO: VICKI SCHWARTZ.

the two higher ones to the left. The route traverses left just below the middle triangle (the lower of the two left-pointing triangles). About halfway up the wall is a wide crack, almost a chimney. The route goes up through this chimney and then curves up and right to a belay just before the start of the traverse, at a left-facing corner. The second pitch traverses left with tremendous exposure (bring a camera!) until below a hemlock, then heads straight to the top. One of the best routes in NJ. FA: before 1975.

15   **The Rib (3 PG)** ★★★   Seventy feet right of Triumvirate is a conspicuous platform at the base of the cliff with a Y-shaped tree. Climb the wide ramp to the top of the cliff. There is a perfect belay ledge with a tree three-quarters of the way up. An idyllic excursion with very enjoyable, continuous and easy climbing. Another Gap classic. FA: before 1975.

One hundred feet right of The Rib platform is an obvious place to set up top-ropes, marked by a triangular roof 20 feet above the trail, then a smaller roof about 10 feet above the trail split by a crack at its right side. There is a small tree 15 feet up the crack. Topropes may be set up by continuing up the trail for 20 feet then scrambling up and back left. Long slings and large camming units will be useful. There are several TR routes here:

16   **Rad Dudes From Hell (12a)** ★   Straight up the prow at the left end of the small roof. FTR: 1989.

17   **Quivering Hips (8)** ★   Overhang and crack at a huge tree close to the cliff.

18   **Last Call Crack (4)**   Six feet right of previous route.

The next climbs are located in the Great Arch, a taller and steeper section of the cliff capped by a line of impressive and intimidating-looking ceilings. For better or worse, these ceilings always appear to shrink as you climb up to them. These routes are best located using the cliff photos in Steele's guide. The dirt platform at the foot of the Great Arch is located 90 paces uphill from the triangular roof just mentioned.

19   **Sobriety Test (7 PG)** ★★   Best 5.7 on Mt. Tammany. Fantastic roof on second pitch. FA: Michael Steele and Randy Seese, late 1980s.

20   **Double Overhang (8– G)** ★★   The first pitch isn't that good but the second pitch features a classic undercling traverse followed by an airy roof with enormous holds. FA: before 1975.

21   **Corkscrew (8)** ★★★   Steele considers this the best route at The Gap. Although we don't go quite that far, it is definitely a classic. The best way to do this route is to combine the last two pitches described in Steele's guidebook. Although the crux overhang at the top allows decent protection, at least one section lower down

on the route will test the nerves of some leaders. Hint: A Lowe-Ball or other small slider is useful. FFA: Hugh Dougher and Ron Matthews, late 1970s or early 1980s.

22   Martin's Fall (6 PG/R) ★   The easiest line up the Great Arch. Has an exciting traverse. FA: before 1975.

23   Tree Toad Fracture (9 G) ★★   This route ascends an immense dihedral which can be seen from far down Rt 80. The dihedral is capped by a ceiling which looks more intimidating from the ground. FA: Dean Giftos and Bill Fontaine, late 1970s or early1980s.

The next two climbs are on a buttress to the right of the Great Arch. Look for a huge overhang penetrated by an obvious weakness (Death Don't Have No Mercy). The overhang is above a grassy slab. At the base is a tree with two trunks, one of which forks.

24   **Denture Grip (8 G/PG)** ★   This route climbs a steep, left-facing wall above a large ledge 40 feet above the ground and to the left of the huge overhang. Great vertical face climbing on quality rock. Difficulty varies according to where you meander. The Extra Strength Denture Grip (5.9) variation is quite exciting since the holds snap after a few seconds of use.

25   **Death Don't Have No Mercy (9+/– PG)** ★★★   This demanding climb threads the weaknesses in an impressive overhanging formation. Despite a spooky and unpleasant start, this is one of the best one-pitch routes at The Gap. Bring many long slings and perhaps double ropes. Some may wish to avoid the poorly protected slab/crack start by climbing the corner to the right. If you clean out and use the moss-filled horizontal at the traverse beneath the ceilings, it is easier. If you boulder across, it is much more intriguing. FFA: Hugh Dougher and Henry McMahon, late 1970s or early 1980s.

26   **War Path (11)** ★   Our final recommendation for the NJ side. Climb the wild overhangs on the remote Indian Head.

MT MINSI (PA SIDE)

All our recommended routes on Mt. Minsi are multi-pitch routes. The routes are listed from right to left as in Steele's guidebook.

The following routes are located on the steep and ominous "Intimidation Wall" at the right end of the Mt Minsi cliffs.

27   **Bird Dog (10a G/PG)** ★★   This steep corner confronts the climber with a continuous barrage of thought-provoking moves. Back up the questionable pins encountered along the way.

28   **Gap View Heights (10c G/PG)** ★★   This route follows another corner just left of Bird Dog. The route is equally steep and

NJAS TOPPING OUT ON TRIUMVIRATE. DELAWARE RIVER IN BACHGROUND. PHOTO: RUTHANNE WAGNER

interesting, but just a bit harder. Again, back up the questionable pins encountered along the way (small TCUs helpful). FFA: Hugh Dougher and Henry McMahon, late 1970s or early 1980s.

29   **Razor's Edge (11a G/PG)** ★★★ This is the most intimidating route at The Gap and the most difficult on the Intimidation Wall. A wild, overhanging corner with long reaches to horizontals. The route is devoid of fixed gear, so prepare yourself for a killer pump placing your own. Double ropes and a three-inch unit are helpful.

30   **High Falls (8+ G/PG)** ★★ This route features a hanging belay followed by a perplexing crux. FFA: Hugh Dougher and Henry McMahon, late 1970s or early 1980s.

The next few routes are at the Land of the Giants, an area overshadowed by huge roofs somewhat reminiscent of the Yellow Wall at the Gunks.

31 **Point of No Return (9– PG)** ★★ This adventurer's climb leads through impressive overhangs and features a long, awkward reach at the crux.

32 **Voyage of the Damned (10c PG)** ★★★ This classic roof has superb buckets and encouraging protection all the way to the lip, but traversing the off-width above is a real struggle. Bring a large cam and double ropes.

33 **Chieftain (8+ PG)** ★★★ This high quality, quintessential Gap route will challenge your protection placement skills. Bring RPs, small cams and a sharp eye for placements.

34 **Surprise (4 P/PG)** ★★ Considered by some to be the finest easy route on Mt. Minsi. It is the best rappel point in the middle of the cliffs (two ropes).

35 **Morning Sickness (11 PG)** ★★ This difficult route sports the first bolt placed at the Gap. Bring a large cam for the horizontal below the roof. Solid 5.12 if climbed while pregnant. FA: Keith Uhl and Jetro Oldrich, 1989.

36 **Raptor of the Steep (10a PG)** ★★ The hardest route on the High Wall. Two difficult moves lead to an exposed final pitch.

37 **Hell and High Water (5 PG)** ★★ This exposed, classic adventure is the longest moderate route on Mt Minsi.

38 **Heroine Hypnosis (5– G)** ★★ The rock on this vintage route is of solid Gunks-like quality.

OTHER RESOURCES Besides Michael Steele's climbing guide, we also recommend the *Hiking Guide to Delaware Water Gap* by N. Miskowski, which is a 1994 revision of an earlier guide by Michael Steele with the same title. This is published by the NY-NJ Trail Conference, GPO Box 2250, NY NY 10116, whose trail maps 15-18 cover the hiking trails along the Delaware from the Water Gap to the NY state line.

DELAWARE WATER GAP (RICKS ROCKS)
North of main Delaware Water Gap climbing areas
50-foot cliff with a few nice moderate lines; Local interest

Ricks Rocks is the name given to a band of 40-foot cliffs along a large ridge within the Delaware Water Gap National Recreational Area. This area is listed separately from the main climbing areas because it is 9 miles to the northeast and is approached quite differently (from Blairstown). The cliffs are similar to those at Mt. Tammany and Mt. Minsi but are much smaller and less appealing. Furthermore, only easy to moderate climbing is possible. There are only a few lines worth doing but one of these is a very nice moderate lead or top-rope. The area is used fairly frequently by a local camp.

ACCESS ISSUES   Climbing at the Delaware Water Gap is an accepted activity known to the park.

DIRECTIONS

Step 1: To get to Rt 602 from:

Rt 94, proceed to Blairstown, then turn north onto Bridge St. / Rt 602. Continue with step 2.

Rt 80W, take Exit 12 for Blairstown and drive north on Rt 521 for 4.7 miles until you come to a T-intersection. Turn left onto Rt 94 / Rt 521 and drive 0.3 mile to the first light. Turn right and immediately take the left-hand fork onto Bridge St. / Rt 602. Continue with Step 2.

Step 2: You will remain on Rt 602 for a total of 5.7M. Proceed to the top of a hill and then turn right onto Millbrook Rd / Rt 602. Continue on Rt 602 for the full 5.7 miles and then park in a semi-circular pulloff on the left. As you proceed along Rt 602, you will see Rick's Rocks up on a large ridge to the left.

Step 3: From the pulloff, follow an obvious, well-maintained path which leads steeply to the base of the cliffs.

THE CLIMBING   Although the cliffs are hundreds of feet long, they are mostly grungy and loose. The best climbing is at the right end where the trail approaches the base. There are several nice moderate lines on an obvious, clean 35-foot face and the arête to the left of it. The obvious crack system on the face can be lead (5.6 G ★★).

A bit further to the left is a conspicuous large dihedral that exits at a pine tree (One Bowl Gully 5.3). Further down is a roof split by a crack (5.7?). Above the roof is a tree with some old slings. Other moderate lines might be possible with extensive cleaning. Nice mixed rock and ice lines materialize when the conditions are right.

CHAPTER 4

SUSSEX COUNTY

ALLAMUCHY STATE PARK (WATERLOO ROCKS)
Near Netcong
Granite slabs and faces up to 40 feet; 22 routes, 5.2 to 5.11, leadable

A group of crystalline granite outcrops in the woods near Allamuchy State Park and Waterloo Village Historic Restoration. Excellent slab, crack and face climbing with leadable routes ranging from 5.2 to 5.11d. The cliffs reach about 80 feet in height although only 40 feet are technical climbing.

ACCESS ISSUES   A special-use permit is presently required to climb in NJ state parks. In the past, only insured commercial guiding services have been able to obtain these permits. In 1996, the NJ state park administrative code will come under review which presents an opportunity to make it more favorable to individual climbers (who vote and pay taxes just like other recreational users!). Since this opportunity will not come again until the year 2000, we recommend writing a letter to your local politicians (freeholders, state senator) and to the Director of NJ State Park Services, CN404, Trenton, NJ 08625.

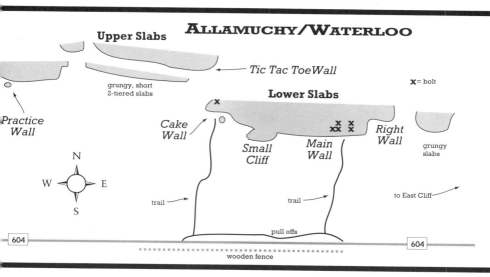

HISTORY   Little is known about the early history of climbing here. NJAS has been climbing here since the early 1970s, but even then there were old-timers who had climbed here for many years. In the late 1980s an active group of local climbers, especially Mike MacDonald, Richard Scheuer, Lucho Romero, Ed Wade and Niel Zandanella cleaned off, occasionally bolted, and led (or top-roped) most of the routes here. As the route names indicate, many of these climbers were not born in the USA!

DIRECTIONS:

Step 1: To reach Rt 604 from:

Rt 80, take Exit 25 (Stanhope/Newton) onto Rt 206N. Continue for about 1 mile and turn left onto Rt 604W (signs here for Waterloo Village and Camp Allamuchy). Continue with step 2.

Rt 206, proceed to a point about 1 mile north of Rt 80 and turn west onto Rt 604 (signs here for Waterloo Village and Camp Allamuchy). Continue with Step 2.

Step 2: Drive west on Rt 604 for 1.7 miles and park at either of two pulloffs on the right side of the road across the street from a wooden fence. From the pulloffs, several trails lead a few hundred feet through the woods to the slabs (see figure). To reach the East Cliff (not shown), walk 200 yards east back along the road from the first pulloff and follow a trail north which leads almost to the cliff.

Recommended Routes   Salty Tears (5.6/5.7+ G/PG), Foreign Invasion (5.9 PG/R), A Year In The Life (5.10a G) plus variations, Blow Out (5.11 G).

The routes are listed from right to left, starting with the East Cliff.

EAST CLIFF

About 80 feet long and 30 feet high, with several conspicuous cracks and two large trees at the base of the slabs. About 200 yards east of the main wall, but it is best reached from the road.

In the late 1980s, this cliff saw a lot of activity, but at the time of writing the moss and lichen have grown back and it needs a thorough cleaning with a wire brush. Some of the best and most difficult routes at Waterloo Rocks are now hidden under this moss. Even the path from the road is overgrown and hard to locate. Excellent ice climbing in the winter.

1   **Spanglish (10 PG)** ★★   One bolt. Slab 10 feet right of rightmost tree at base.

2   **(7 G)**   Crack midway between two trees at base.

3   **B.I.T.U.S.A. (Born in the USA) (11 G)** ★★   Climb seam then face behind left tree. Protection in crack to left.

4   **(7 G)**   Crack just left of tree. The blank face between this route and the next probably still awaits a first ascent.

5   **Muddy Waters (8 G)** ★   The next and very conspicuous crack to the left. The smaller cracks just to the left of this are of lesser interest.

6   **(7 G)**   The crack 6 feet right of European Vacation.

7   **European Vacation (9+ R)** ★★   This is the leftmost climb on the East Cliff, and goes up the slab a few feet left of the arête, staying slightly left of an old bolt with no hanger. This marks the end of the main slab; to the left of it are some blocky overhangs.

RIGHT WALL

A short face, with vertical cracks, just right of the main wall. There is an easily accessible tree at the top of this for top-roping.

8   **A Touch Too Much (10 R)**   Walk 20 feet right from the right end of the right wall and up the hill 30 feet to a rear wall, also facing south, with a small tree growing out of the face. Climb to top staying right of tree.

9   **(8+ PG)** ★   The double crack at the extreme right end of the Right Wall. 30 feet.

10   **(7+ PG)** ★   The left-most crack just right of Blow Out. 30 feet.

11   **Blow Out (11 G)** ★   Two bolts. Steep face just right of right-facing corner. Gear is useful above second bolt. 30 feet.

WATERLOO

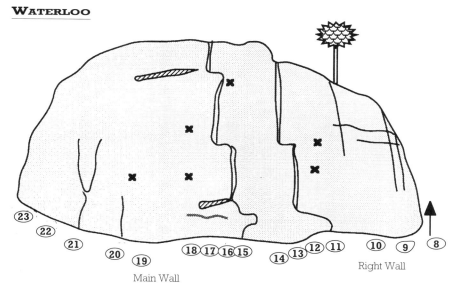

Main Wall

Right Wall

12   **(5 PG)**   Right-facing corner separating Right Wall from Main Wall. 30 feet.

13   **(8 PG)**   Arête to left of right-facing corner. 30 feet.

MAIN WALL

Largest wall with the best climbing.

14   **(7 PG)** ★★   Enjoyable climbing on face between two large right-facing corners. 35 feet.

15   **(5 PG)**   One bolt. Climb tiered right-facing corner system which begins 12 feet above ground. 35 feet.

16   **(6)**   Top rope. Arête just left of right-facing corner. 35 feet.

JOHN MCELDOWNEY TOPROPING ON MAIN WALL (ROUTE 14) AT WATERLOO ROCKS. PHOTO: SUSANNA CUYLER.

17   **A Year in the Life (10a G)**
★★   Two bolts. Approach first bolt from good holds on right and clip it. Traverse left onto blank face (away from any good holds on right). Head for the next bolt (crux), then the top. Small cams and nuts useful above second bolt. 60 feet.

18   **Direct Start to A Year in the Life (11d)** ★   Climb bleak, bouldery face directly up to first bolt without using any good holds on or near corner to right. Pre-clipping first bolt recommended. 60 feet.

19   **Another Start to A Year in the Life (10d)** ★★   Begin several feet left of direct start, and climb delicately up and right on small holds. Pre-clipping first bolt recommended. 60 feet.

20   **Foreign Invasion (9 PG/R)** ★   One bolt. Start at a small left-facing corner and climb face past single bolt. The gear higher up is better than it looks, but be careful on the exciting runout just above the first bolt because a fall would deposit you extremely close to the ground, if not on it. Bring small cams and nuts. 60 feet.

21   **Hourglass (8 R)** ★   Begin at vertical crack about six feet left of Foreign Invasion. Climb through hourglass crack formation, then past several small corners to top. 60 feet.

22   **(7 R)**   Climb face staying left of Hourglass at all times. Bottom is run out. 60 feet.

23   **(6 G)**   Climb up through notch in overhang about 12 feet left of Hourglass.

24   **(V2/V3)**   The main wall can be traversed in either direction.

To the left of the main wall the base of the cliff rises and the rock is less steep. After about 30 feet some large right-slanting overhangs can be seen.

25   **(2 PG)**   Starting under the right end of the overhangs, climb easily up, step right, then up easy slabs to the top. Stay well away from the overhangs. 80 feet.

26   **(7–)**   Traverse from left to right under overhangs.

SMALL CLIFF

A detached block some 30 yards west of the main wall, about 20 feet wide and 12 feet high.

27   **(7?)**   Toprope right side of face.

28   **(8?)**   Top rope. Climb face just left of center.

Behind the Small Cliff the base of the wall rises to a platform with two large trees, below some 30-foot high slabs. This is about 100 feet left of the main wall.

29   **Ego Hexentric (11d)**   Top rope. Face behind leftmost of the two trees.

30   **Stomach Hair Face (10c)**   Top rope. Ten feet left of previous route.

CAKE WALL

A narrow section of clean rock, at the far left end of the Lower Slabs (100 yards left of the main wall). There are two large trees at the base. There is a bolt at the very top, but use a tree for an anchor instead.

31   **Flash Appeal (11)**   Top rope. On the right side of this wall is a right-facing wall capped by an overhang. Climb through hang. Harder now that a key hold has broken.

32   **(6 G)** ★   Start behind tree near base. Climb straight up to crack which starts above small overhang. Jam or layback crack to stance. Either continue straight up passing bolt on right or traverse left to flake and then climb to top. 30 feet.

33   **(9 PG)**   Start behind left-most tree near base. Move up and slightly left to small overhang. Climb straight up blank-looking face

to stance. Continue straight up at flake or traverse left and climb blankest part of slab (5.7). 30 feet.

34   **(5 PG)**   Start behind left-most tree near base. Move up and left to skirt blank-looking face on left. Traverse a bit right and climb flake to top. 30 feet.

TIC TAC TOE WALL

Sixty yards directly uphill from the Cake Wall is a section of clean rock with a low overhang six feet off the ground. Several climbs pull over this overhang and finish with a delicate slab move. A toprope is easily anchored to a tree at the top.

JIM MCGRATH TOPROPING THE CLASSIC *A YEAR IN THE LIFE* (LEFT START, ROUTE 19) AT WATERLOO ROCKS. PHOTO: RUTHANNE WAGNER.

35   **Raincoats and Candles (7 G)**   Crack at far right end of this section of wall.

36   **Toe (9– R)**   Start below right end of low overhang at dirty vertical crack. Climb up and left. 25 feet.

37   **Chin Chaver (10a R)**   Start below center of low overhang at jutting, tapering horizontal hold that feels hollow to touch. Grunt and heave over awkward overhang. 25 feet.

38   **Stoke the Locals (9+ R)**   Start below left end of low overhang at large jutting hold about 4 feet right of an arête. Without using arête, climb to top. 25 feet.

39   **(2 G)**   Start in large, obvious left-facing corner. Climb up, move out onto arête and proceed up crack. 25 feet.

40   **(3 G)**   Start as with previous route, but climb up left through crack in roof. 25 feet. Thirty feet farther to the left is a nice slab with easy bouldering.

PRACTICE WALL

About 100 yards left of the Tic Tac Toe Wall, at the far left end of the Upper Slabs, is a clean low-angle slab. This slab has a bolt near the top, a tree growing out of the middle and two stout trees near the base.

41   **(9+)**   Top rope. Climb through overhang directly behind R-most tree and continue straight to top. 25 feet.

42   **(4 PG)**   Start at right-slanting crack which starts at face-level about 8 feet right of tree growing near base. Climb straight up to stance. Step left. Pass on right side of tree growing out of cliff and continue to top. 25 feet.

43   **(3 PG)**   Start directly in front of tree near base. Climb obvious crack system straight to top. 25 feet.

44   **Salty Tears (6/7+ G/PG)** ★   Start directly beneath bolt. Climb up to bolt and clip it. The natural inclination here is to follow better holds on right side of bolt (5.6). For contrived 5.7+ variation, stay left of bolt and right of arête (without using it). 25 feet.

45   **(5 PG)**   Arête left of Salty Tears.

There are a number of other cliffs in this park that could be developed. For example, the higher tiers that can be found a long way above the Tic Tac Toe Wall. At the far west end of the park is an outcrop known as The Monolith where there is said to be excellent climbing.

HIGH POINT STATE PARK

25' metaquartzite cliff; Several moderate routes; Local Interest

Small rock face next to the Appalachian Trail just south of the High Point Monument, the highest point in NJ. The rock is Gunks metaquartzite, and the not-quite vertical cliff is 25 feet to 30 feet high. The cliff faces east and is slow to dry.

ACCESS ISSUES   A special-use permit is presently required to climb in NJ state parks. In the past, only insured commercial guiding services have been able to obtain these permits. In 1996, the NJ state park administrative code will come under review which presents an opportunity to make it more favorable to individual climbers (who vote and pay taxes just like other recreational users!). Since this opportunity will not come again until the year 2000, we recommend writing a letter to your local politicians (freeholders, state senator) and to the Director of NJ State Park Services, CN404, Trenton, NJ 08625.

DIRECTIONS   Heading north on Rt 23, enter High Point State Park, and after about a mile park in the designated but inconspicuous Appalachian Trail (A.T.) parking lot on the left. If you miss the parking lot, 200 feet further on Rt 23 brings you to the Park Office on the left and the entrance road to the High Point Monument on the right. Go back.

From the furthest (southwest) corner of the parking lot, walk west for 50 feet and turn left on the A.T. (white blazes). Follow the A.T. past a painted pipe sticking out of the ground, where red- and yellow-blazed trails cross the A.T. Ignore these and stay on the A.T. After about five minutes of walking the cliff will appear on the right side of the trail.

All difficulty ratings are estimated—until we climb here on a dry day! The routes are described fom right to left.

1   **(6??)**   Attractive crack with good protection, just right of center of face.

2   **(10??)**   Crack left of center.

3   **(5??)**   Dihedral at left side of cliff.

4   **(4??)**   Lumpy face on far left.

Other lines would be possible with cleaning. There are additional possibilities on the cliffs further along the ridge to the left. There is good ice climbing here in winter.

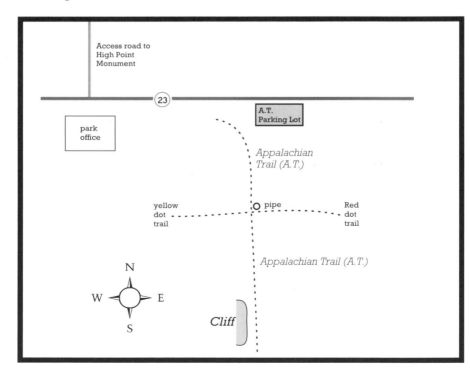

CHAPTER 5

MORRIS COUNTY

GREEN POND

Near Craigmeur Ski Area and town of Green Pond
Puddingstone cliffs; 25 routes, 5.0-5.10, 1-2 pitches, leading

The rock at Green Pond is "pudding stone," a sandstone conglomerate. The cliff height averages from 75 to 100 feet. Climbs are short, usually one or two short pitches. With a well-rounded rack, the protection is generally adequate, although there is much loose rock (see Hazards). Fourth-class trails can be used for descent or one can rappel down. Trails at the base and the top (100 yards back from the edge) run the full length of the cliff.

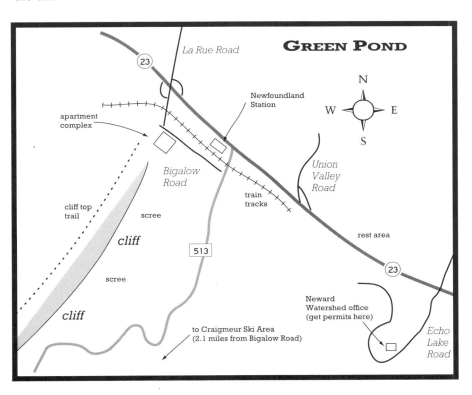

GREEN POND (FAR RIGHT). PHOTO:VICKI SCHWARTZ.

ACCESS ISSUES   WARNING! The land is owned by the Newark Watershed which requires that you have a hiking permit to be in the area. Permits and parking decals can be obtained from the Newark Conservation and Development Corp., located about a half mile from Rt 23 on Echo Lake Rd (see map below).

The authors are not aware of any explicit policy on climbing although this does not guarantee that such policy does not exist. You must take full responsibility for your own actions. This guidebook describes potential climbing resources but does not imply in any way that you have permission to use those resources for climbing or any other purpose. You alone are responsible for determining whether any form of recreational activity is permitted. If climbing is not permitted, the recommended response is to comply fully, but at the same time, to form an activist organization to lobby for open access.

HISTORY   Although the history of climbing at Green Pond is largely unknown, one can infer from the old pins found on some of the routes and the commanding position these cliffs hold over the surrounding landscape

that climbers have visited the area for decades. Steve O'Keefe wrote the first and only guidebook in the early 1980s, which we have re-worked, with Steve's permission, to create this chapter. The route names are taken from O'Keefe's guidebook.

HAZARDS   The rock conglomerate here never metamorphised, and this cliff can be very loose and very dangerous. Wear a helmet, certainly, but also be prepared for unexpectedly large rocks to fall apart as you pull or step up on them. Rescue would be difficult because of large boulder fields below the cliffs. Leaders should therefore stay within their limits. The ratings given in this chapter have had little verification and should be taken lightly. Also, beware of wasps, hornets, chiggers and poisonous snakes.

DIRECTIONS   Take Rt 23 in the direction of Rt 513 and the Craigmeur Ski Area. Park near the apartment complex on Bigelow Rd, just south of the Newfoundland train station, as shown in the map.

The easiest approach is as follows: Follow the blue trail which starts by the apartment complex until you come to two V-shaped trees with blazes on them, and two dead logs between them. Angle left to the cliffs. This places

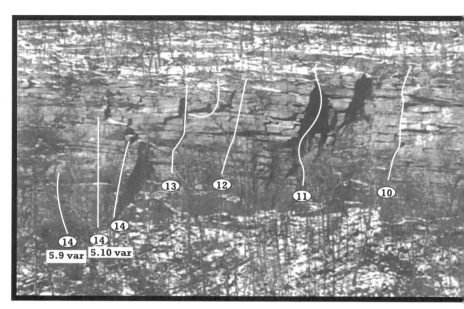

GREEN POND (NOT SO FAR RIGHT). PHOTO:VICKI SCHWARTZ.

you at a fourth-class gully next to Gaston at the right end of the Center Wall. Look for a large block at the top of the cliff which is near the finish of Gaston.

The climbs are listed from right to left facing the cliff.

RIGHT WALL

One can descend from these climbs by rappeling down the face to the right of Red Fuzz. A rappel can also be made on the left side of the Dog Leg buttress (75 feet) followed by a scramble to the bottom. The first two routes are not shown in the cliff photos.

1   **Red Fuzz (4)**   Up left-facing corner to trees, continue up small corner crack to overhang, step right and up gully to belay.

2   **Zig-Zag (6)** ★★   P1: Up small inside corner facing left to below chimney, step right then left to ledge in chimney crack (awkward), continue to top of chimney and traverse left to belay ledge with pine tree. P2: Follow jam crack up open book 20 feet to overhang, traverse right to small tree and up, continue up slab and through notch above.

3   **Dog Leg (3)**   To get to the start of this climb, scamble up easy rock left of a large buttress (there is a prominent crack running horizontally to the corner). P1: Scramble up to trees below broken

NEW JERSEY • MORRIS COUNTY

chimney crack, climb chimney to tree, step right around corner, then traverse right and slightly up to belay on corner. P2: Up broken rock heading slightly left, finish up crack in a white 15-foot wall.

5.4 Variation   P1: Climb up ten feet to large ceiling, traverse right under ceiling (ancient fixed pin) and around corner to belay at pine tree. P2: Diagonal up left to tree, step right up face to ledge (standard route's belay ledge) and continue to top.

5.3 Variation   Located right around corner from 5.4 start is another crack, 5.3, that can be climbed. Remainder of first and second pitch same as 5.4 variation.

4   **One Move (8)**   Start at log at base of crack in bulge (old pin in crack 15 feet up). Climb the crack, then traverse off left.

5   **Frog's Head (4/5)**   Climb a broken right-facing corner to the top. Loose rock.

SPACE SWING WALL

This area begins just left of a prominent right-facing corner in the middle of the cliffs. Scramble up to a large ledge for start of climbs. A third-class descent trail starts here, angles up and right, then back left to the top.

6   **Unnamed Route (3/4)**   Start same as Space Swing or at crack 15 feet to right. Climb up to ledge, walk right to chimney. Up this and follow corner to top. Crumbly and loose.

Green Pond (Center Wall). Photo:Vicki Schwartz.

7   **Space Swing (9/10)** ★   Up corner to tree, step left onto outside
     corner, step back right and up white rock to small overhang. Climb
     overhang to ledge, then up left over overhanging "visor." A
     strenuous climb that is usually top-roped. Those that fall off will
     understand the name of the climb. The climb can be recognized by
     the large square block on the belay ledge.

8   **Mad Dog Special (6/7)**   Start to the left of Space Swing just right
     of large graffiti. Up vegetated groove or slab for 15 feet to inside
     corner facing left. Up this, step right and up face to tree. Climb up
     and left to small inside corner facing right below left side of
     overhang. Climb up and step right above overhang. Good
     protection. Numerous variations in the 5.8 to 5.9 range have been
     climbed to the left and right of this route .

9   **Blowout (10/11)** ★   Start below impressive off-width roof crack.
     Climb face and step left to clump of trees. Follow crack up to big
     roof, then out the roof crack to top. Can be lead with large nuts.

10   **Copperhead (2)**   Start at large, left-facing, broken corner left of
     Blowout and right of large recessed gully. Climb left-facing wall on

left side until level with tree, step right and climb crack and face to the top. Loose rock.

CENTER WALL

This area begins left of a large, recessed gully (referred to in the directions for the approach). For Body Snatcher and nearby routes only the first 30 feet up to a ledge are worth doing and can easily be top-roped.

11 **Gaston (4)**   Start left of recessed gully at large right-facing inside corner with several large off-width cracks in it. Up loose rock to ledge, step left and climb squeeze chimney on right-facing wall (tight unless you have a small head). At top of chimney, step out right onto large ledge, then climb corner or face on left to top.

12 **First 9 (9/10)** ★   Start slightly left of jam crack in small roof 30 feet above ground. Follow flakes up and slightly right to tree below roof crack. Surmount the roof crack, then climb the face above. Crux is short and well protected

13 **Roundabout (8)** ★   Starts to left of First 9 by another overhang with a bent tree 15 feet below it. Up face to bent tree, step right and climb up to below overhang (one can also go left around tree, harder). Climb up right over the overhang and follow inside corner to the top.

Variation   After climbing the first overhang, follow the inside corner to a second overhang. Traverse right beneath the second overhang to a break, then climb to the top.

14   **Body Snatcher (9)**   Crux is ten feet off the ground. Start at ramp which slants up and right to a small overhang. Climb ramp and past overhang to a ledge. Step right and climb face to a large ledge. Step left and continue up to tree on right. From there, one can scramble right and down fourth class corner to trail. 5.9 and 5.10 TR variations have been climbed just to the left of Body Snatcher.

15   **Vick's Fall (8)**   Climb the face to the right of a recessed gully.

16   **Goldlines Are Free (3)**   Continuing left from Body Snatcher, the trail rises slightly. Just before the trail begins to descend slightly, scramble up and left until below a large roof. Climb up crack and corner to the top of the block (or start to right in right-facing corner). Move right and up to ledge, then follow inside corner to the top.

5.10 TR Variation ★   At top of block, step left and follow crack through ceiling.

DETACHED BUTTRESS AREA
Begins at a large detached buttress.

17   **Short Face (5)**   Climb a nice face and crack just right of center on the detached buttress.

18   **(Class 4)**   Scramble up to left side of large detached buttress. Scramble 12 feet up chimney to ledge, walk right around corner, and up a small fourth-class face to top.

5.0 Variation   Again start by scrambling up small chimney. Up this past trees, follow corner to ledge. From here one can step right and belay or continue up face and corner to top. Can be used to descend the cliff.

TR Variation   The face to the right of the corner makes a nice short top-rope.

19   **Old Route (4)** ★   Start 200 feet to the left of large detached
     buttress at groove with small chimney 40 feet above ground. P1:
     Up groove (much loose rock) and through chimney (fixed pin).
     Step left and continue up face to large ledge near top of cliffs. P2:
     Walk right until below overhang (fixed pin), climb this and follow
     corner above to the cedar on top. Can be done in one pitch.

20   **Leaning Pillar (4)**   P1: Climb loose right-facing corner, traverse
     left and around corner to belay near large pine tree. P2: Up face
     past bulge with old pin to large ledge, climb up left and then up
     face on left side of overhang. A bit loose in spots. First pitch
     overgrown.

LEFT WALL

To the left of Leaning Pillar the trail becomes faint, so follow the base of the
cliff. The Left Wall area begins at a prominent buttress extending halfway to
the top with a large chimney to the left. One can rappel from the trees near
the edge at the top.

21   **Go For It (9)** ★   P1: Climb off-width jam crack on right-facing
     wall, step left and climb corner to ledge. P2: Step left, climb
     overlap to ledge (old pin) and continue to top.

22   **Big Chimney (5)**   Up right-hand side of chimney, traverse left
     and follow steps on inside corner to top. Usually wet. Not
     recommended although it climbs conspicuous feature.

23   **Wrist (4)** ★   Start below first right-facing corner to left of Big
     Chimney. Follow crack in face to ledge, then follow right-facing
     corner to its top. Step out left and climb diagonally left up face to
     top.

24   **(3)**   Climb left-facing corner which is just right of right-facing
     corner. Loose and overgrown at bottom. Not recommended.

25   **Nick's Line (8)**   Climb large right-facing inside corner left of
     Wrist. Often wet. Poor protection and loose rock. Not
     recommended.

26   **Rodeo (9/10)** ★   Start below center of large roof which
     continues for 300 feet. P1: Up the crack and small face on left to
     ledge. Continue up face to a large ledge. P2: Step left and ascend
     crack in face to overhang, follow crack out right and around
     corner, then follow inside corner facing right to top. FA: 1978. FFA:
     Steve O'Keefe,1981

27   **Aid Roof (4 A2)** ★   This route surmounts the long roof at a crack
     near the left end. Up face and corner past small tree to detached
     block. Continue up crack and follow this through 12-foot overhang,
     then follow corner to top. FA: 1978

CRAIGMEUR SKI AREA

More cliffs are visible behind the Craigmeur Ski Area. No more is known.

PYRAMID MOUNTAIN PARK

Near Boonton
Great hiking with a few interesting boulders along the way

A nature park recently established by the combined efforts of citizens' groups, conservation organizations, corporations and government agencies. The park is best known for the outrageous Tripod Rock, an enormous boulder precariously balanced on three much smaller boulders. There are many excellent hiking trails which ascend steep and rocky territory. The best trails are described in *Fifty Hikes in New Jersey,* by B Scofield et al, Backcountry Publications, 1988 (Hike #16). This is a good place to go for a hike with your "significant other" if you want to impress him or her with your bouldering prowess.

ACCESS ISSUES The authors are not aware of any explicit access policy although this does not guarantee that such policy does not exist. You must take full responsibility for your own actions. This guidebook describes potential climbing resources but does not imply in any way that you have permission to use those resources for climbing or any other purpose. You alone are responsible for determining whether any form of recreational

RUTHANNE WAGNER BOULDERING ON TRIPOD ROCK, PYRAMID MOUNTAIN PARK. PHOTO: RUTHANNE WAGNER.

activity is permitted. If climbing is not permitted, the recommended response is to comply fully, but at the same time, to form an activist organization to lobby for open access.

DIRECTIONS   From Rt 287N, take Exit 44 (the second exit north of US 80) for Main Street, Boonton. Proceed west on Main Street for a few blocks and turn right onto Rt 511 N. Roughly 4 miles of driving brings you to the park.

From Rt 23, exit at Rt 511 / Boonton Ave in Butler and drive a few miles south to the park.

The visitors center and parking lot are on the west side of Rt 511. A trail map, obtainable at the visitor's center, shows all the blazed hiking trails as well as the names and locations of the interesting boulders. The white trail is the most direct way to get to the boulders, but it is also the least interesting since it follows an uninspiring and unshaded field beneath power lines.

Come here only if you are primarily interested in hiking. Leave your chalk bags, harnesses and ropes at home because the park will not appreciate them. The trail map shows five places that seem like they might have climbing:

1 **Cat Rocks**—Not much here.

2 **Tripod Rock**—A two-hundred ton boulder impossibly balanced on three tiny boulders. Getting to the top at all in sneakers is a problem in itself. There is also potential for several one-move or two-move extreme problems and a circular traverse. Be careful, however, not to tip the boulder off its tripod! Tripod Rock is believed to have had spiritual and astronomical significance for the Lenape Indians.

3 **Bear Rock**—A massive and quite impressive boulder about 20 feet high and 40 feet long which marks the boundary between Kinnelon and Montville boroughs. Bear Rock features a thin vertical face, steep arêtes, an almost featureless overhanging face and a slab with a troublesome undercut start. The height of the boulder makes some of the potential problems committing. A few of the best and safest problems are:

The Prow (V1) ★   Start low on overhanging arête near tree. Climb arête to gain incredible jugs, do one-arm hang for 10 secs on each arm, then either drop or climb down.

Hellacious Flake (V5) ★   On side of boulder facing wooden footbridge, use conspicuous layback flake to surmount undercut start and gain slab above.

4 Whale Rock—Smaller boulder with potential for bouldering in the V0-V2 range.

5 Eagle Cliffs—Not much here.

TOURNE COUNTY PARK (THE TOURNE)

Near Mountain Lakes [Morris County]
Granite boulders; 32 problems V0-V4

Numerous granite boulders in a quiet and peaceful park with good jogging trails and scenic views of surrounding areas. The Tourne is a wooded mountain about 900 feet above sea level. Early Dutch settlers called it the "Torren," which means tower. New York City can be seen from the top on a clear day. The park is locked at dusk.

ACCESS ISSUES   The authors are not aware of any explicit access policy although this does not guarantee that such policy does not exist. You must take full responsibility for your own actions. This guidebook describes potential climbing resources but does not imply in any way that you have permission to use those resources for climbing or any other purpose. You alone are responsible for determining whether any form of recreational activity is permitted. If climbing is not permitted, the recommended response is to comply fully, but at the same time, to form an activist organization to lobby for open access.

Discretion, minimal impact, and safe, responsible conduct are extremely important here. Visitors to the park pass by the boulders all the time. Do not bring any climbing equipment or attempt to set up ropes. Anything beyond safe scrambling and bouldering will only jeopardize access. The Downwind Boulders are particularly exposed to view and should be avoided, especially on weekends.

DIRECTIONS   Going north on Rt 287, cross Rt 80 and take the next exit, which is Exit 43, Intervale Rd. At the end of the ramp, turn left, cross Rt 287 and turn right at the first light onto Fanny Rd in Mountain Lakes. At this point, you should already have seen the first of a number of signs which lead you to the park. In any case, proceed 0.95 mile to the second stop sign on Fanny Rd where it intersects The Boulevard and Elcock Ave. Turn right on Elcock Ave and almost immediately turn left at a fork onto Powerville Rd. After about 0.2 mile turn left onto McCaffrey Lane near a large sign for the park. Proceed 0.6 mile to the second parking lot (near ball field) and park your car. To reach the boulders, head north up the stairs near the parking lot entrance (following signs for scenic overlook). After passing the restrooms on the left, look for the Downwind Boulders uphill.

HAZARDS   Beware of black flies. Some spots have dense poison ivy but this can be avoided with a little care. For some problems, a spotter is recommended because of thin, crumbly holds or unpleasant landings. Problems from which you must not fall have been given an R rating, but as always you must rely on your own judgment.

RECOMMENDED ROUTES   Flytrap (V0+), Stinger (V1), Mouse Cradle Lunge (V2), Fannyscraper Traverse (V4).

The boulders and problems are listed from south to north. Although the Downwind Boulders are the first you will encounter, the best place to start is at the Blackfly Convention Boulder which has a number of smooth, enjoyable problems with good holds.

DOWNWIND BOULDERS

On the hill above the toilets, these boulders are quite exposed to view and should be avoided on weekends and when the park is crowded. The largest boulder has several big horizontals and contains the first problem. The roughly trapezoidal boulder to the right of this and the outcrop behind the trapezoidal boulder contain additional problems.

1   **(V0–)**   Climb discontinuous vertical seam up center of large boulder with big horizontals. 15 feet.

2   **(V0)**   Climb slab up the front of trapezoidal boulder. Spotter recommended. 13 feet.

3   **(V0+)**   Start a few feet right of previous problem and just left of inside corner formed by trapezoidal boulder and smaller boulder to right. Climb up and left to top. Smaller boulder is off-route. Spotter recommended. 13 feet.

4   **(V0–)**   Start behind trapezoidal boulder, just below and right of V-notch formed with adjacent boulder. Climb short, thin face to top. 9 feet.

5   **(V0)**   Start at 3-inch shelf-like hold near left end of outcrop. Climb up and slightly left to top. Spotter recommended. 10 feet.

6   **(V0+ R)**   Start just left of obvious ledge. Climb onto left side of ledge. Continue straight up thin rock to top. Spotter recommended. 14 feet.

7   **(V0)**   Climb nose-like arête just uphill and left from previous two problems. Rocks embedded in ground are off-route. 12 feet.

IVY BOULDER

One-hundred-and-fifty feet north of the Downwind Boulders is a 10-foot-high boulder with an overhanging east side, surrounded by lesser boulders. Warning: Beware of poison ivy.

8   **(V0–)**   Right-slanting crack just left of big immobile rock, which is off-route. 10 feet.

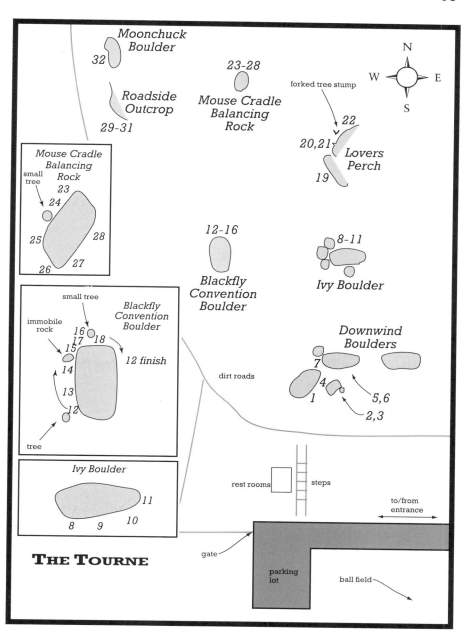

THE TOURNE

9   **(V0–)**   From directly in front of big immobile rock (off-route), climb straight up. 10 feet.

10   **(V0–)**   Start right of big immobile rock below right-leaning, almost horizontal crack. Hand traverse right to lip of boulder and continue around until your feet touch ground on opposite side of boulder. 11 feet.

11   **(V0–)**   Start beneath overhanging end of boulder and pull up and over. 9 feet.

BLACKFLY CONVENTION BOULDER

One-hundred-and-fifty feet west of the Ivy Boulder is an isolated boulder in the shape of a slightly squashed egg. Many of the problems are described in relationship to a large immobile rock embedded in the ground next to the boulder at an overhanging bulge.

12   **Fannyscraper Traverse (V4)** ★★   A right-to-left traverse of the steep side of the boulder. Start just right of flat undercut near tree and perform low traverse left until you can reach up to incut holds just below lip by small tree (at Short and Stupid problem). At this point, you have joined Popgun Traverse which is followed to the end. At least one foot should be just above ground at all times and you'll be virtually scraping your fanny on the large immobile rock

PN ON THE *FANNYSCRAPER TRAVERSE,* TOURNE COUNTY PARK. PHOTO: RUTHANNE WAGNER.

when passing the crux bulge. The sloping shelf-like holds above the crux bulge are all off-route. All the elements of a fantastic traverse are here: creative body positioning and a combination of power and endurance. 33 feet. FKA: Paul Nick, 1995.

13   **Flatulence (V0)**   At flat undercut, crouch down and start from holds just above undercut. Reach for jugs, then hoist yourself past slopers to top. 11 feet.

14   **Flytrap (V0+)** ★   Sit down on right side of large immobile rock. Reach up and place hands on rightmost two of three protruding jugs, position your feet on boulder and fire up vertical face to top. 10 feet.

15   **Stinger (V1)** ★   Sit down on left side of large immobile rock. Stretch up and place right hand on highest and left-most of three protruding jugs. Position your feet on boulder, shoot up over steep bulge, then contend with irritating slopers on top-out (bailing off to side is wimpy). 10 feet.

16   **Swarm (V0)**   Start halfway between large immobile rock and small tree, hang from 1.5-inch shelf-like hold about 5.5 feet above ground, position your feet on boulder, and go straight up. 10 feet.

17   **Popgun Traverse (V0+)** ★   Start same as Swarm and shoot up left to incut holds just below lip near small tree. Traverse left until incut holds end, then continue left along slopers around corner to finish. Never reach over top. Problem also serves as final pumpy sequence on Fannyscraper Traverse. 15 feet.

18   **Short and Stupid (V0–)**   Start at small tree, reach up to good holds just below lip and climb straight up and over top. Easy. 8 feet.

LOVER'S PERCH

About 300 feet north-northeast of the Blackfly Convention Boulder is the largest outcrop in the park. There is a lot of easy climbing and scrambling here. Only the more interesting problems are listed. (PN: Hopefully, you won't disturb the lovers the way I did one evening while blithely pulling over the top.)

19   **(V0)**   Climb thin seam directly up steepest, tallest part of detached southwest face. 14 feet.

20   **(V0–)**   Arête to left of detached southwest face (just right of corner crack). 14 feet.

21   **(V0–)**   Corner crack. 14 feet.

22   **(V0)**   Slight arête in front of forked tree stump (just left of mossy dihedral and just right of big flake). Rule: Hands can touch only holds on or immediately next to arête but feet can go anywhere. 13 feet.

MOUSE CRADLE BALANCING ROCK

About 250 feet northwest of Lover's Perch is a boulder balanced a foot off the ground near one end.

23   **(V0–)**   Face 5 feet left of small tree. 8 feet.

24   **(V0–)**   Face just left of small tree. 9 feet.

25   **(V0)**   Climb flakes several feet right of small tree at rounded outside corner. 9 feet.

26   **(V1)** ★   Climb left side of arête past slopers to top. 9 feet.

27   **Mouse Cradle Lunge (V2)** ★   Step onto thin, slightly overhanging face and lunge to top (good dyno practice!). Left edge of boulder is off-route, but good left-hand sidepull two feet from left edge is fair game. Leaping to top from ground receives partial-credit. Helps to be a basketball player. 9 feet.

28   **(V0)**   Sit-down start just right of Mouse Cradle Lunge. Place hands on big jug, place feet on boulder, then fire up right to top. 9 feet.

ROADSIDE OUTCROP

About 300 feet west of Mouse Cradle Balancing Rock is an outcrop overlooking a dirt road.

29   **(V0–)**   Obvious big crack just left of tree. 12 feet.

30   **(V0 R)**   Climb up just right of tree. Bad landing. 12 feet.

31   **(V2 R)**   Start 8 feet right of tree at low overhang. Reach up for holds and climb straight up to top without touching corner to left or rock to right. Tricky. Bad landing without spotter. 13 feet.

MOONCHUCK BOULDER

This boulder, just north of the Roadside Outcrop, resembles the posterior of a stone giant.

32   **(V1 R)**   Climb blank-looking dome. Tenuous top-out on crumbly crystals with grim landing. 14 feet

CHAPTER 6

PASSAIC COUNTY

NORVIN GREEN STATE FOREST (PINE PADDIES)
Near Wanaque Reservoir and town of Wanaque
50' vertical faces, cracks; Routes 5.3 to 5.12, some leading; Traverses to V5

The forest near the Weiss Ecology Center contains at least three climbable cliffs in an area known as the Pine Paddies, so called because of the high concentration of pitch pines in the area. The rock is a conglomerate of reddish pudding stone and quartz crystals. The main cliff, several hundred feet long and up to 50 feet high, can be lead or top-roped. Three routes in particular are NJ classics with good protection and a fair degree of difficulty (5.8, 5.8+ and 5.11d). Numerous other top-rope routes and difficult traverses present additional challenges. The main cliff tends to remain wet for a day following rain. A nearby shorter cliff, 60 feet long and 10 to 15 feet high, has a few short top-rope lines and some easy bouldering. From the main cliff, one can also bushwack for five minutes to a slab known as the Pizza Face which has low angle routes up to 90 feet long, suitable for beginner leads or top-ropes.

ACCESS ISSUES   A special-use permit is presently required to climb in NJ state parks. In the past, only insured commercial guiding services have been able to obtain these permits. In 1996, the NJ state park administrative code will come under review which presents an opportunity to make it more favorable to individual climbers (who vote and pay taxes just like other recreational users!). Since this opportunity will not come again until the year 2000, we recommend writing a letter to your local politicians (freeholders, state senator) and to the Director of NJ State Park Services, CN404, Trenton, NJ 08625.

Use discretion and do not carry climbing equipment out in the open, especially when near the Weiss Ecology Center.

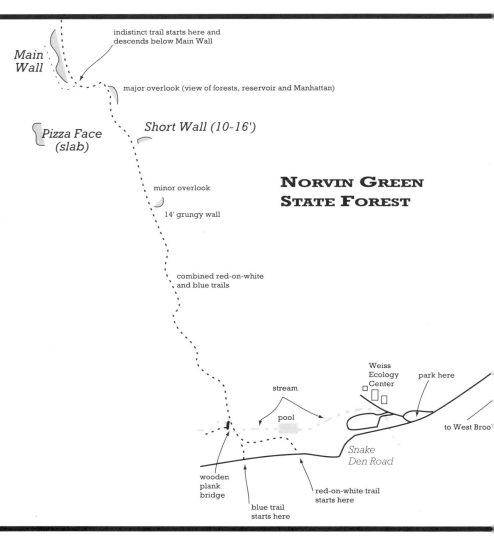

CLIMBING HISTORY   Little is known of the climbing history at the Pine Paddies other than that climbers have come here for decades. We were told by a local climber that the route OOBLIK (5.11d) was aided in 1976 and freed on top-rope several years later. Two pins from the original ascent are still on the route and two additional pins were added for a free lead, probably in recent years.

DIRECTIONS   From Rt 287N, take Exit 53 for Bloomingdale—Pompton Lakes (just north of exit for Rt 23 and far north of Rt 80 intersection). From the exit, turn right onto Hamburg Turnpike (following signs for Rt 511 ALT).

Proceed for 0.6 mile and turn left onto Ringwood Ave / Rt 511. Proceed north on Ringwood Ave for 5.1 miles passing through the town of Wanaque (after 1.25M, Rt 511 turns left by an overpass but continue straight ahead on Ringwood Ave). Turn left onto West Brook Rd (Wanaque Reservoir appears here). Proceed 1.9 miles, crossing a bridge and staying left at a fork. Turn left onto Snake Den Rd (just past Townshend Rd) and proceed 0.6 mile, staying left at fork, to the Weiss Ecology Center parking lot which is on the right. Park here. On some weekends the Ecology Center charges a modest parking fee.

Do not walk through the Weiss Ecology Center. Instead, hike up Snake Den Rd for a fifth of a mile to the start of the blue trail on the right and follow this into the woods (see map). About 150 feet from the road, the blue trail merges with the red-on-white trail. The blue trail is known as the Hewitt-Butler Trail, while the red-on-white trail is the Wyanokie Circular Trail (Hike #11 in the *Fifty Hikes in New Jersey*). The trails in this area are covered by the NY-NJ Trail Conference Map #21.

Follow the combined red-on-white and blue trails for about 20 minutes. Look for a 10- to 15-foot wall with bright, clean rock on the right side of the trail. Several routes are listed for this wall. About 300 feet further, at the highest point on the trail, is an overlook on the right with scenic views of the reservoir. On a clear day, Manhattan can be seen on the eastern horizon. The forests stretch to the horizon in all directions and it is hard to believe you are in NJ. A little further, the trail curves left to an overlook on the left side of the trail. You are now at the top of the main wall which is below the overlook. If you look around here, you may discover the remains of several old bolts. You can also see the pinnacle next to the Depression (see topo). Hikers have been known to step across onto the pinnacle and eat lunch there. The easiest descent is to the left when facing outward.

HAZARDS   Many of the rock edges are sharp and abrasive. If top-roping, make sure the rope runs cleanly and that any knots in runners are not rubbing against the rock. Also, avoid Tarzan-like swings from your top-rope.

Copperheads and rattlesnakes have been spotted in the area. Beware the eponymous snake den!

The black flies here can be particularly vicious.

The hike to the cliffs is about a half-mile. Bring extra water and a first aid kit.

The red-on-white trail sees a reasonable amount of traffic on weekends. Beware of kids throwing rocks from the top of the cliff.

RECOMMENDED ROUTES   Brave New World (5.8 G), Count Crackula (5.8+ G), OOBLIK (5.11d G), Dislocator Traverse (V3+).

Only worthwhile lead climbs have been given a protection rating. All other routes are designated TR and should not be led because of insecure rock and poor protection. A rescue would be slow and difficult because of the remote location.

SHORT WALL
This is the short, clean 10- to 15-foot wall on the right side of the blazed trail.

1   **(V0–)**   The right half of the wall has some easy bouldering. The most interesting line climbs straight up a few feet right of a dead tree, which is the middle tree of three trees next to the wall.

2   **(7)**   Top rope. Climb the obvious dihedral which divides the overhangs on the left half of the wall.

3   **(10a)** ★   Top rope. Start about five feet left of the main dihedral (on the left side of a nose). Climb up, traverse slightly right, and then climb back left through small, awkward, notch to top. Short route reminiscent of the Near Trapps.

PINE PADDIES: MAIN WALL
The main wall is illustrated with two topos. The first shows the left half of the main wall (everything left of the Depression, the large recess in the center of the cliff). The second shows the Depression and the right half of the main wall.

Main Wall: Left Half

4   **Practice Wall (1 to 3)**   Easy climbing and bouldering up to 25 feet.

5   **(8)**   Top rope. Directly behind a sycamore tree is a steep face with a shallow, indistinct crack system which zigzags up to the top.

6   **Son of Schnicklefritz (8)**   Top rope. Six feet right of a sycamore tree is an alcove below a diamond pattern formed by slanting cracks. Climb directly out top of alcove and continue to top. Easier variations can be done by climbing out right side of alcove.

7   **Brave New World (8 G)** ★★★   Start to right of alcove at bottom of big right-rising ramp. Pull up at obvious, clean, left-slanting crack and continue up zigzagging cracks with good protection to top. Belay at pine tree directly above route.

8   **Polkacide (8+)** ★   Top rope. Start to right of big right-slanting ramp at some vertical cracks behind tree. Climb cracks for ten feet and then follow right-slanting crack to ledge. Step left to rusty pin and climb vertical seam/crack to top.

9   **(5)**   Climb big left-slanting crack to ledge.

10   **OOBLIK (11d G)** ★★   Climb thin vertical seam with four pins up to ledge. Either continue to top or belay on ledge and scramble back left to ground. Clearing the small overhang near the start is a

tricky challenge. Two of the pins are a bit old, but at least they are closely spaced.

11 **Project (13?)** A dark waterstreak looks exceptionally bleak even when dry, yet a series of small edges might make it possible.

12 **Count Crackula (8+ G)** ★★ Great fingercrack with superior jams.

The next three routes are short toprope problems on the thin face to the right of Count Crackula.

13 **Jason Goes To Hell (12a?)** Top rope. Start seven feet right of fingercrack at slight water streak. Formulate a "pain minimization sequence" up sharp, excruciating holds aiming for tiny, short right-facing corner about 14 feet up and 5 feet to left of start. Continue to top.

PN on *BRAVE NEW WORLD*, NORVIN GREEN STATE FOREST. PHOTO: RUTHANNE WAGNER.

NORVIN GREEN: MAIN WALL LEFT HALF

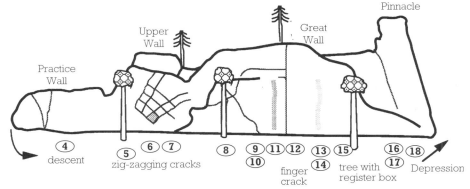

14   **In Hell 'Twas I (11b)**
Top rope. Start one foot
right of Jason. Climb
sharp, painful holds to
gain small, short right-
facing corner about 11
feet above ground.
Continue up vertical seam
to top.

15   **In Held 'Twas I (10c)**
Top rope. Start three feet
left of register box tree
with your right hand on
good flake. Climb more or
less straight up and pull
onto left slanting ramp
(crux) just below where
ramp becomes short
right-facing vertical
corner.

16   **Project (V5)**   Traverse
from right-facing ramp all
the way left to left-facing
ramp. Your feet should not
rise more than five feet
above ground.

17   **The Sprout (3)**   Climb
easy ramp which slants up
and left.

PN ON *COUNT CRACKULA*, NORVIN GREEN
STATE FOREST. PHOTO: RUTHANNE
WAGNER.

18   **Pinnacle Power (8)** ★   Top rope. Climb crack on left side of
pinnacle. At top of crack, traverse right and climb exposed outer
face of pinnacle to top. Near top, use right-hand arête for
handholds. To anchor toprope, put protection in deep crack
splitting top of pinnacle and drop rope a few feet to side of crack.

Main Wall: Right Half

19   **(0)**   Easy chimney at left side of Depression.

20   **(10c)**   Top rope. The wall in the back of the Depression appears
interesting from the ground but the few holds on the mid-height
face simply snap off in your hands. It is possible to start farther right
with your left hand at a vertical seam and then climb up and left to
the top. The climb is okay, but the difficulty of setting up a toprope
probably exceeds the rewards.

21 **(V3–)**   Start just to left of tree growing 1 foot from cliff at right end of Depression. Traverse right about 30 feet to easy ground at left-slanting ramp. Stay just above ground or ledges. All easy ledges near ground are off-route. Sequential in a few spots, awkward and grueling.

22 **Darth Vader (6 PG/R)** ★   Climb large corner system forming right side of Depression. The corner slants awkwardly near start. The protection is good once the corner system becomes vertical. A direct-start variation (5.8 or 5.9 TR) begins to left of tree and climbs straight up face, joining the regular route where the corner system becomes vertical.

23 **Skywalker (12a?)**   Top rope. Start as with Darth Vader. Climb up to where Darth Vader corner system traverses left, but instead move up and right to ledge below steep face. Climb left side of steep face to top.

24 **The Nose (9)** ★★   Top rope. Start below rounded arête (i.e., the nose) between Darth Vader and arching ceiling of Peanut Gallery. Several variations are possible, but the best one is as follows: Climb vertical crack up to stance beneath nose. Skirt nose on left to gain left-facing corner. Climb corner halfway until some holds allow you to traverse right onto nose itself. Climb nose to stance on top of nose. Continue up steep rock to the top. An easier variation follows left-facing corner on left side of nose to its top and traverses right to top of nose.

25 **Peanut Gallery (9?)** ★★   Top rope. Climb left-facing corner formed by large flake up to prominent left-arching ceiling. Traverse left beneath the ceiling and continue to top.

Direct Variation (10?)   Climb over the ceiling instead of traversing left.

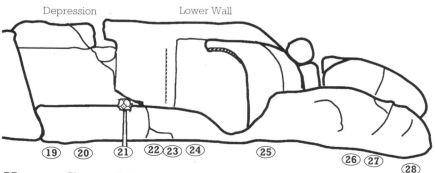

Norvin Green Main Wall: Right Half

Indirect Variation (10?)   Climb initial corner a few feet and follow a system of flakes moving left and up.

26   **Cake Flake (4)** ★   Top rope. Climb large, obvious, right-pointing flake and continue to tree at base of chimney. Climb chimney a few feet and then step right to exposed position just above overhang. Continue to top. This could be an exciting and steep beginner's route, but beware of loose rock.

27   **Wookie (10?)** ★   Top rope. Start about 5 feet right of Cake Flake at some obvious underclings 6 feet above the ground. Climb straight up slightly overhanging face to overhanging block above. Climb block at obvious crack which divides it.

Variation (9?)   Start a few feet further to right at a short right slanting crack. Follow the crack up and right. Approach the overhanging upper block about five feet right of obvious crack which divides it and layback large flake to top.

28   **Dislocator Traverse (V3+)** ★★   Begin near right end of cliff at lowest dip in trail. Start at very short right-slanting crack and perform low traverse about 40 feet left past Cake Flake to easy ground at small left-rising ramp. Stay just above ground and use only bottom nine feet of wall. Good problem requiring a combination of endurance, body positioning and power. If you're short, expect trouble.

PIZZA FACE

This is worth looking at because it is a large expanse of climbable rock. The obvious routes are easy, and although slightly harder climbing can be done on the left, most climbers will not find anything challenging. The trail map shows the location of Pizza Face which is a few minutes from the main wall. Some scouting around may be needed to find it.

GARRET MOUNTAIN RESERVATION

Near West Paterson
Moderate bouldering on 10-12' vertical trap rock outcrops; Local interest

Popular park located on top of Garret Mountain. The bouldering is in an area known as Rocky Hollow. The problems are pleasant and enjoyable with good landings. The difficulty does not exceed V0+ although the problems are consistently thin and vertical. The park also contains 150-foot cliffs facing the east but climbing is forbidden on them.

ACCESS ISSUES   Roped climbing on any of the cliffs in the park is strictly prohibited. The authors are not aware of any explicit access policy regarding bouldering on the short and relatively harmless outcrops described in this chapter although this does not guarantee that such policy does not exist. You must take full responsibility for your own actions. This

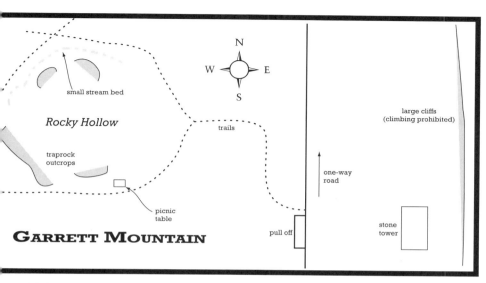

guidebook describes potential climbing resources but does not imply in any way that you have permission to use those resources for climbing or any other purpose. You alone are responsible for determining whether any form of recreational activity is permitted. If climbing is not permitted, the recommended response is to comply fully, but at the same time, to form an activist organization to lobby for open access.

DIRECTIONS From the GSP heading north, take Exit 153B to Rt 3W. Proceed for a few miles and then, just before the intersection with Rt 146, follow signs to Valley Rd. If approaching from GSP heading south, instead take Exit 154, follow Rt 146W for a few miles, and take the exit for Valley Rd. Either way, proceed north on Valley Rd for 1.8 miles. At the intersection of Valley Rd, Fenner Ave and Mountain Park Rd, make a very sharp left turn onto Mountain Park Rd. Proceed uphill for 0.35 mile and turn right into the park entrance. Proceed straight into the park on a one-way road for 0.6 mile and park at a pulloff on the left below a stone tower which is uphill on the right. The one-way road circles the park for 2.0 miles and then rejoins itself right at the entrance/exit. If you miss the stone tower, you will have to complete the 2-mile circle. The trap rock outcrops are downhill on the left side of the road as shown in the figure below.

HAZARDS Nothing serious, just the usual broken glass, poison ivy, brambles, mosquitoes, black flies,....

1 (V0–) Face left of vertical crack.
2 (V0–) Face right of vertical crack and left of small protruding buttress.

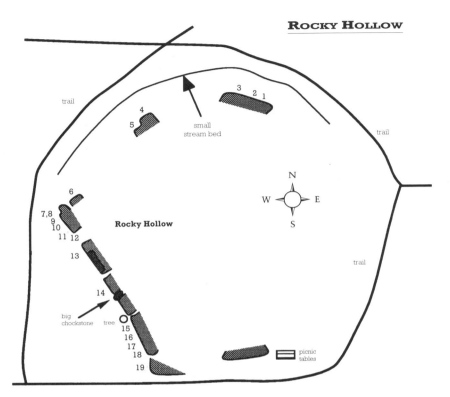

3   **(V0–)**   Small protruding buttress near right end of outcrop. Use only front of protrusion.

4   **(V0–)**   Center of face to left of corner and crack which split boulder.

5   **(V0–)**   Center of face to right of corner and crack which split boulder.

6   **(V0–)**   Climb short thin boulder at Barb+Al graffitti.

7   **(V1+)**   Traverse entire wall from left to right without touching ground or top (except where wall is obviously too short). 150 feet.

8   **(V0–)**   Face left of left-facing corner and crack.

9   **(V0+)**   Climb thin face between corner on left and vertical seam on right without touching either.

10   **(V0–)**   Vertical seam.

11   **(V0)**   Face right of seam.

12   **(V0–)**   Arête.

13   **(V0–)**   Face left of ledge.

14   (V0+)   Climb thinnest part of face left of big natural chockstone.

15   (V0+)   Climb face just right of tree (without traversing right to bigger holds).

16   (V0+)   Climb tiny seam (L of bigger seam) using only holds near seam.

17   (V0+)   Bigger seam.

18   (V0)   Face just left of chimney.

19   (V0–)   Climb rightmost face staying just left of center.

Several burly roof problems can be found near the park exit onto Mountain Park Rd. They are worth a quick stop. Park in the very last pulloff on the right, just before the circular park road rejoins itself at the exit/entrance. Walk 35 feet into the woods on the right.

20   (V0)   Climb north-facing roof. When your hands reach top, slide right and mantle over right end of roof.

21   (V0) ★   Left side of steepest part of west-facing roof.

22   (V0)   Right side of steepest part of west-facing roof.

RIFLE CAMP PARK

Near West Paterson
Moderate bouldering (up to V0+); Short TR routes; Local interest

On Garret Mountain, a few miles south of Garret Mountain Reservation. The climbing here consists of moderate bouldering (V0- to V0+) and a few short toprope routes (15 feet high). The outcrops are not as clean nor as much fun as those at Garret Mountain Reservation, although they are quieter and more secluded. On the east side of the park there are extensive cliffs up to 100 feet high but they are very loose and virtually fourth class. Moreover, climbing is forbidden on them.

ACCESS ISSUES   Climbing any of the large cliffs in the park is strictly prohibited. The authors are not aware of any explicit access policy regarding bouldering on the short and relatively harmless outcrops described in this section although this does not guarantee that such policy does not exist. You must take full responsibility for your own actions. This guidebook describes potential climbing resources but does not imply in any way that you have permission to use those resources for climbing or any other purpose. You alone are responsible for determining whether any form of recreational activity is permitted. If climbing is not permitted, the recommended response is to comply fully, but at the same time, to form an activist organization to lobby for open access.

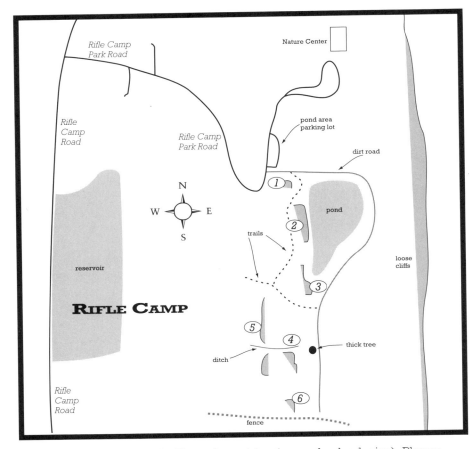

HAZARDS   Loose rock. Fierce brambles (green barbed wire). Planes taking off from Teterboro Airport just to the east (a twin-engined jet crashed into the park on May 24, 1988, killing four people on board).

DIRECTIONS   A visit to Rifle Camp Park is recommended in combination with a visit to Garret Mountain. To reach Rifle Camp Park from the pulloff below the stone tower in Garret Mountain Reservation, continue along the one-way road for 0.85 mile and exit the park on the right through a gate. Turn left. Proceed for 0.3 mile and turn left onto Rifle Camp Rd. Drive south for 0.6 mile to the park entrance on the left. Note: to return to Rt 46 or Rt 3 from here, continue south on Rifle Camp Rd for 1.3 miles and follow signs.

To reach Rifle Camp Park directly from the GSP: If heading north, take exit 153B to Rt 3W, drive a few miles, and turn onto Rt 146 W. If heading south on GSP, instead take exit 154 to Rt 146W. Either way, from Rt 146W take the

Great Notch exit and go north on Rifle Camp Rd for 1.3 miles to the park entrance on the right.

From the entrance, proceed into the park for about 0.5 mile and park on the right in the Pond Area Parking Lot. There is a dirt road next to the parking lot which leads to the pond (see figure).

1   Small 10-foot outcrop has several problems up to V0+.

2   Twenty-foot outcrop overlooking the pond can be top-roped with routes approaching 5.11 on the far left. The rock is overhanging, broken and loose. There are often lots of people around the pond.

3   Outcrop with a dead tree leaning against it. Has some V0- bouldering and a small roof up above a ledge. An uncompleted problem is to hand traverse from right to left with hands above the roof but below the top, and with feet on the wall below the roof. With some cleaning and a spotter (loose hold), it should go at about V3.

4   Vertical wall 15-feet high and 60 feet long, excellent for top-roping. The obvious crack is about 5.7, the seam to the left is about 5.9, and the face next to it is a bit harder. The whole wall can be traversed.

5   Extensive line of outcrops up to 15 feet with V0– to V0 bouldering.

6   Fourteen-foot-high outcrop in shape of a large corner. Nice V0– to V0 bouldering.

ROB BIENKOWSKY TOP-ROPING ON THE MAIN
WALL AT MILLS RESERVATION. PHOTO: MIKE
BEAGEN.

CHAPTER 7

ESSEX COUNTY

MILLS RESERVATION
Near Upper Montclair
45' trap rock cliff; Nice TR routes, 5.5 to 5.10a; Bouldering V0-V2

Quiet and secluded neighborhood park. The best climbing is on a 45-foot vertical basalt cliff at the south (or left) end of the park, about 200 yards from the road. The cliff overlooks houses at the edge of the park. Out of courtesy to the neighbors do not scream or yell from the top of the cliff. Natural top-rope anchors are scarce so bring a selection of camming units and long slings or a spare rope. There is a lesser cliff hidden at the north (or right) end of the park, and nice bouldering next to Cedar Grove Reservoir (similar to Rocky Hollow on Garret Mountain).

ACCESS ISSUES   The authors are not aware of any explicit access policy although this does not guarantee that such policy does not exist. You must take full responsibility for your own actions. This guidebook describes potential climbing resources but does not imply in any way that you have permission to use those resources for climbing or any other purpose. You alone are responsible for determining whether any form of recreational activity is permitted. If climbing is not permitted, the recommended response is to comply fully, but at the same time, to form an activist organization to lobby for open access.

DIRECTIONS   From the GSP take Exit 151, follow Watchung Ave west for 2.1 miles (there is a tricky pair of dogleg turns passing the Watchung Ave train station) to the T-junction with Upper Mountain Ave. Turn right, then second left (Bradford Ave) then first right (Highland Ave), go 0.55 mile, do a U-turn and park on the left side of the road next to a "Mountain Park Nature Trail" sign.

Follow the Nature Trail uphill (west) for 200 yards to the green-dot trail, turn left and walk 200 yards. The main cliffs are visible uphill on the right. The climbing wall is near the left end. For the small cliff, turn right instead of left at the green-dot trail and walk 300 yards. The trail passes directly below the small cliff.

For the Cedar Grove Reservoir bouldering, continue north on Watchung Ave for 0.5 mile to Normal Ave, turn left, continue 0.3 mile and turn right on Reservoir Dr just before the reservoir. Reservoir Dr, used extensively by joggers, is normally closed to cars, so park at the barrier and jog along the road for about a quarter-mile. The outcrops are just off the right side of the road and cannot be missed.

THE MAIN WALL   45 FEET

The major features are a large crack in the center of the wall and a roof about 25 feet left of the crack. Most of the routes begin with a boulderish start over a small overhang about six feet above the ground. The routes are usually top-roped.

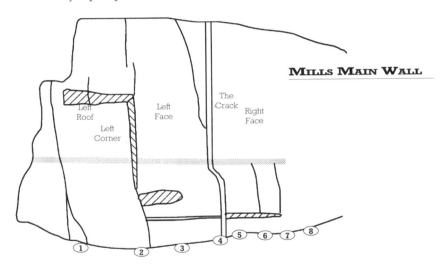

1   **Left Roof (9) ★★**   Start 5 feet to the left of left-facing corner, beneath roof. Climb up to center of roof, clear it at small seam and continue up thin face to top.

2   **Left Corner (8+) ★★**   Climb conspicuous left-facing corner up to right side of roof. Continue straight up thin face above to top. Nice face climbing above roof.

3   **Left Face (7/7+) ★**   Climb face anywhere between Left Corner and The Crack. Hardest variation pulls directly over overhang near start.

4   **The Crack (5)**   Climb conspicuous crack.

5   **Right Face Direct (10a) ★**   Three feet right of The Crack, boulder the overhang at a groove and continue up steep face to top.

6   **Right Face Direct Variation (8) ★**   Six feet right of The Crack, pull over overhang at crack and continue up face to top.

7   **Right Face (7) ★**   Start 10 feet right of The Crack at right end of overhang. Climb face to top.

8   **Icey EB's (4)**   Small crack slightly uphill and to right of main face.

THE SMALL CLIFF 18 FEET

A few interesting toprope lines surmount the overhang on the left side of the small cliff.

9   **(9)**   Clear center of overhang at small right-facing layback corner.

10   **(10a)**   Clear right end of overhang at vertical crack.

11   **(5)**   Climb moderate face several feet right of vertical crack.

CEDAR GROVE RESERVOIR

Most of the bouldering here is moderate V0 but several problems are more challenging. A toprope is appropriate for the taller problems.

12   **(V0)**   Climb short, thin face eliminating chimney on left and outside corner on right. 9 feet.

13   **(V1)**   Traverse entire wall without touching ground or top. 150 feet.

14   **(V0–)**   Climb thinnest part of face just left of big corner. 8 feet.

15   **(V0–)**   Short crack. 9 feet.

16   **(V0–)**   Bear-hug up right side of arête. 11 feet.

17   **(V0–)**   Thinnest part of wide face. 11 feet.

18   **(V0–)**   Taller face just left of conspicuous crack. 17´ feet.

19   **(V0)**   Climb thin face just right of crack without using crack. 17 feet.

20   **(V0) ★**   Left side of arête. 17 feet.

21   **(V1 R) ★**   Start up jugs on right side of arête, then up a few thin moves to the exciting top-out. Arête on left is off-route. 17 feet.

22   **(V2) ★**   Climb thin face halfway between left edge of face and flake/seam system on right. Eliminate holds within 1.5 feet of left edge of face. Flake/seam system is also off-route including good foothold in seam near ground. Slightly contrived, but worthwhile. 14 feet.

23   **(V0–) ★**   Flake/seam system in center of face. 14 feet.

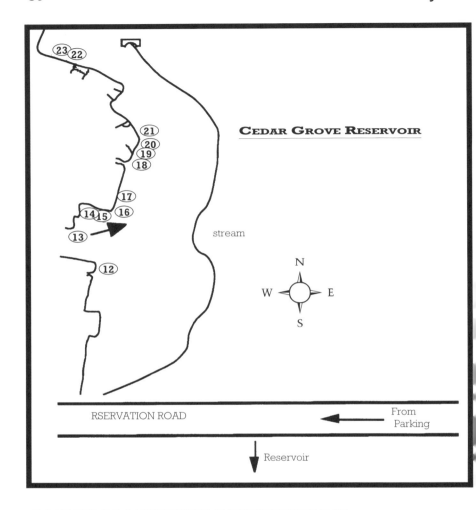

SOUTH MOUNTAIN RESERVATION

South Orange
15-20' basalt cliffs; Short TR routes up to 5.10; Local interest

Basalt trap rock cliffs and outcrops up to 20 feet high are scattered throughout this extensive reservation. Two locations are of special interest to climbers:

Hemlock Falls Cliffs line both sides of a picturesque waterfall in the center of the South Mountain Reservation. Hemlock Falls is similar to Watchung, except that the cliffs are smaller with easier climbing and the rock is a bit more crumbly. However, this location is quiet and peaceful on weekdays. On weekends, the spot should be avoided because of the crowds of picnickers. This guide lists 18 routes at Hemlock Falls. Most routes are easy to moderate.

Turtle Back Rock Near Turtle Back Zoo in the northeast corner of the reservation is a basalt outcrop with a decorative tortoise-shell pattern. This outcrop features a nice overhanging wall with some cracks and seams reaching 5.10 in difficulty. If only this was taller! The outcrop is above a busy and noisy road and is more secluded when the trees have their leaves.

According to the leaflet describing the Turtle Back Nature Trail (*Turtle Back Rock Interpretive Trail,* Center for Environmental Studies, 621 Eagle Rock Ave., Roseland, NJ 07068, circa 1982), it is not known whether the intriguing tortoise-shell pattern on this outcrop is natural or if it was carved by the Unami branch of the Lenni Lenape Tribe, who dwelled here until the 17th century and honored the turtle.

[Debate: Are the patterns natural? NJAS: We have necessarily spent hours with our faces only inches from this rock, and it seems apparent that these patterns are man-made. Among other reasons, the patterns follow the outlines of the blocks and so are of recent origin. They also occur on faces with many different orientations, which would not be so if they were produced by erosion. PN: Sounds logical; however, the small trap rock outcrops on Garret Mountain (also included in this book) feature similar patterns but which are less distinct and less "tortoise-like." You, the reader, can decide!]

ACCESS ISSUES The authors are not aware of any explicit access policy although this does not guarantee that such policy does not exist. You must take full responsibility for your own actions. This guidebook describes potential climbing resources but does not imply in any way that you have permission to use those resources for climbing or any other purpose. You alone are responsible for determining whether any form of recreational activity is permitted. If climbing is not permitted, the recommended response is to comply fully, but at the same time, to form an activist organization to lobby for open access.

DIRECTIONS

Step 1: To get to Milburn Ave from:

Rt 78 East, take Exit 49B (just before GSP) onto Springfield Ave (Rt 124). Very shortly, turn left onto Valley Rd via a right-hand jug handle (signs for Valley Rd point the way). Continue for several blocks to the second stoplight and turn sharply left onto Millburn Ave West. Continue with step 2 below.

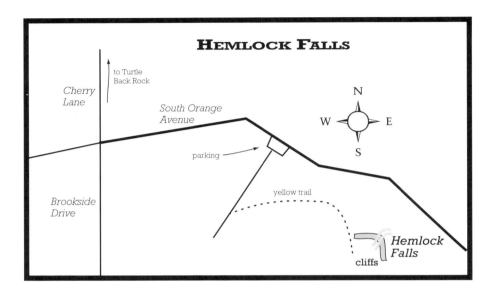

Rt 78 West, take Exit 50A (just east of the GSP) onto Vaux Hall Rd. Continue for several blocks and turn left onto Millburn Ave West. Continue with step 2 below.

GSP, take Exit 142 at the Union Toll Plaza onto Rt 78W. From Rt 78W, take Exit 50A onto Vaux Hall Rd. Continue for several blocks and turn left onto Millburn Ave West. Continue with Step 2 below.

Step 2: Continue on Millburn Ave West for several blocks. Then shortly after Millburn Ave West curves right and becomes Essex St, turn right onto Lackawanna Pl. At the T-intersection, turn left on Glen Ave. After 0.2M, make the first right onto Brookside Dr. which brings you into the reservation.

Step 3: To get to Hemlock Falls, continue on Brookside Dr for 1.8M. Turn right on South Orange Ave (Rt 510) and proceed east for 0.4 mile to a small parking area on the right (which is not accessible from W-bound lane). Walk about 600 feet southwest along the obvious trail, then turn sharply left onto another trail with yellow trail markers. Continue for a fifth of a mile to Hemlock Falls.

Step 4: To get to Turtle Back Rock from Brookside Dr north, continue on Brookside Dr which becomes Cherry Lane after crossing South Orange Ave. Take Cherry Lane to the next traffic light and turn right onto Northfield Ave. Proceed east on Northfield Ave for 0.5M. On Northfield Ave, you will pass the Turtle Back Zoo and South Mountain Arena on the right and further along at 0.4M, you can spot Turtle Back Rock above the right side of the road. Turn right at a light onto Walker Rd. Drive 0.3 mile and turn right into the reservation parking lot. Park in the near right-hand corner of the parking lot (see map). Follow a pleasant nature trail with trail markers which starts in the parking lot corner and actually crosses the top of the Turtle Back Rock (see map). Alternatively, follow a more direct dirt road and turn right onto the first trail which crosses the dirt road (ignore trails which end at the dirt road).

HAZARDS   Loose rock, broken glass, and poison ivy. Warning: The short and moderate nature of some of these routes may tempt some climbers to climb unroped. However, be warned that this rock is extremely friable and holds have been known to break.

HEMLOCK FALLS

1	(0)	Easy chimney.
2	(1)	Climb up a few feet right of chimney.
3	(4)	Small crack.
4	(0)	Another easy chimney.
5	(2)	Outside corner just right of chimney.
6	(5)	Surmount bulge about 12 feet up.
7	(7)	Climb up and through groove between two tiny arêtes. Loose rock.
8	(5)	Climb up a few feet left of left-facing corner. At thin section near top, angle left and up.
9	(2)	Left-facing corner.
10	(5)	Start just right of tree and climb up angling slightly left to top.
11	(7)	Climb crack passing tree on left without touching it.

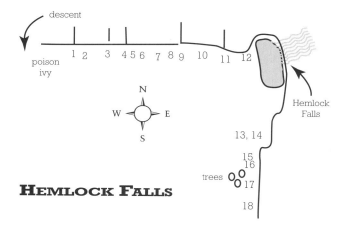

HEMLOCK FALLS

12   (6)   Climb arête.

13   (9) ★   Thin-looking vertical face just left of left-facing corner.

14   (10d) ★   Climb same thin vertical face but without reaching left for tempting jug near top.

15   (7)   Start at edge of dirty drop-off. Traverse left a few feet above drop-off and climb face to top.

16   (8)   Climb face a few feet left of clump of trees.

17   (9+) ★   Start just right of clump of trees. Climb steep face to lifesaver tree at lip. Exciting boulder problem for the competent.

18   (8)   Start about 6 feet right of clump of trees at big knob-like hold. Climb up to lip and hand traverse right to escape nasty top-out.

TURTLE BACK ROCK

19   (8/9+)   Short steep face gets harder as you move right.

20   (9)   Thin seam with puzzling start. 18 feet.

21   (7)   Three-inch crack behind tree.

TURTLE BACK ROCK

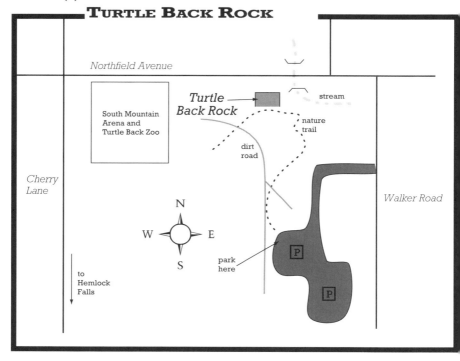

22   (9)   Mantle onto ledge and climb vertical seam which ends at ledge and short right-facing corner.

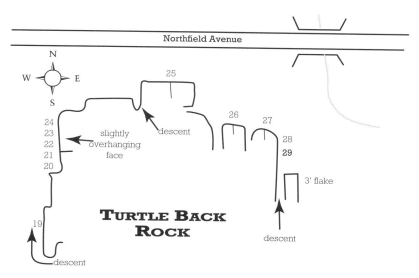

23 (10d) ★ Climb face 3 to 4 feet left of vertical seam from previous problem. With difficulty, top out through slight, rounded depression without reaching right for good holds near seam and corner.

24 (10a) ★ Start below some vertical seams immediately right of tallest part of face. Mantle onto ledge, climb seams, and top out at tallest point.

25 (5) ★ Nice 2-inch crack with introductory hand jamming.

26 (8–) Dirty, awkward 6-inch crack. Harder than it looks.

27 (8+) ★ Dirty 6-inch crack. Harder than it looks. Requires a lot of tenacious groping and hand jams.

28 (10b) Start crouched beneath overhang at right side of 15-foot-wide wall. Staying within a few feet of right-hand arête, clear overhang and continue to top.

29 (4/5) Moderate face climbing on left half of 15-foot-wide wall.

JEFF GRUENBERG TOPROPING HIS ROUTE *MICROFACE* AT WATCHUNG.
PHOTO: DOUG ALLCOCK.

CHAPTER 8

UNION COUNTY

WATCHUNG RESERVATION (SEELEY'S ESCARPMENT)
Near Scotch Plains
20- to 30-foot basalt cliffs; TR routes 5.6 to 5.11; Bouldering V0-V2, 150-foot traverse

Two cliffs, both 20 to 30 feet high and 150 to 200 feet long, overlook Diamond Hill Rd at the far west end of the Watchung Reservation. This is an excellent top-rope and bouldering area. The routes are mostly strenuous, vertical face climbs in the 5.8 to 5.11 range. Triple Overhangs (5.10d), in the center of the upper cliff, is a classic by any standards. The overhanging upper cliff is often dry in damp weather.

These cliffs are part of the Watchung Mountains. The name is Indian (Wach Unks = High Hills). Although these "mountains" are only 879 feet high at their tallest (at High Mountain), they account for several other areas in this guide: Garret Mountain, Mills Reservation, Rifle Camp Park and South Mountain Reservation. The rock at these areas is gabbro, a form of basalt, also known as trap rock. Gabbro has a high coefficient of friction, dries quickly and, despite some break-away holds, is ideal for climbing—it is rightly called "the best of all God's rocks"

ACCESS ISSUES (CLIMBING PROHIBITED!): Although this is one of the oldest and best-known climbing areas in the state, climbing has been forbidden here for several years, and "No Climbing" signs are posted at all access points. However, it appears (at the time of writing) that the combined efforts of the Watchung Area Rock Climbers Organization (WARCO), presently headed by Jeff Lucas, The Access Fund and others, will soon result in this area being opened to climbing. For this reason, and because of its historical importance, we have decided to include Watchung in this guidebook. Until the area is reopened, however, do not climb here, as this could sabotage the negotiations. To join or receive information on WARCO, write to WARCO, 22 Lexington Road, Basking Ridge, NJ 07920.

HISTORY One of the regulars at Watchung, Vic Benes, started climbing here in 1967. He says that when he began, there were people who already had been climbing here for 15 years. So there is a history of at least 40 years of technical climbing at these cliffs. In *The New York Walk Book* (New York-New Jersey Trail Conference, 232 Madison Ave, New York NY 10016, 1984) there is a sketch of the cliffs, drawn in 1948, which clearly shows people scrambling on the rocks at the upper cliff. Vic Benes and NJAS are part of a long tradition of Bell Labs climbing here. It is very likely that Bill Shockley (co-inventor of the transistor, Nobel Lareate, and climber of Shockley's Ceiling at the Gunks) practiced here in the mid-1950s. In 1975, Russ Raffa established the area's first hard classics, Triple Overhangs (5.10d) and the Credit Card Climb (5.11).

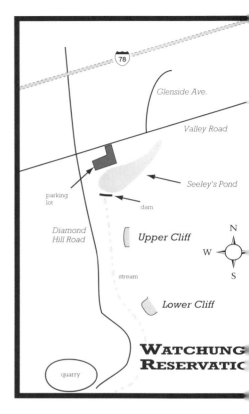

DIRECTIONS To reach the Seeley's Pond parking lot from...

Rt 22 East: take the exit for Rt 78, follow the jughandle across Rt 22 and onto Diamond Hill Rd. Follow this through a traffic light, past a quarry on the left, and then to the next light. The cliffs can be seen on your right before reaching this light. At the light, turn right onto Valley Rd and take the next right into the parking lot.

Rt 22 West: take the exit for Rt 78 and turn right at the next traffic light onto Diamond Hill Rd. Continue to the next light (the cliffs can be seen on your right before reaching this light). Turn right onto Valley Rd and take next right into the parking lot.

Rt 78 East: take Exit 43 (New Providence-Berkeley Heights), turn right onto Glenside Ave and follow it to a T junction with Valley Rd. Turn right and take the next left into the parking lot.

Rt 78 West: take Exit 43 (New Providence-Berkeley Heights) which puts you onto Diamond Hill Rd going in the wrong direction. Make crux U-turn, go back down the hill to a traffic light and turn left on Valley Rd. Take next right into the parking lot.

Park in the far corner of the lot, walk south past the pond and cross the stream below the dam. Then follow the left bank for a few hundred feet until you see the upper cliff. The lower cliff is about 500 feet south of the upper cliff.

Occasionally the stream is too high to cross after heavy rain. In this case it is possible to park further up Valley Rd and follow trails south and then southwest around Seeley's Pond to the upper cliff.

HAZARDS   Broken glass and empty beer cans. The base of the cliff would be knee-deep in broken bottles by now, if it wasn't for climbers regularly hauling out sack-loads of trash. Liz Allcock, who fortunately is a professional nurse and had a first aid kit handy, once had to remove a 1/2" splinter of glass from NJAS's thumb (impaled while doing the traverse).

Teenagers partying at the top of the cliff. There is a story that one climber proposed a rule that if a drunk falls off the cliff, the carcass should be carried down and placed by the side of the road, to make it look like human "road-kill." Needless to say, the authors completely disassociate themselves from this view.

Loose rock. Several major holds break off each year—a sound argument against soloing.

Cliffs are exposed to a noisy main road, especially when the trees lack leaves.

Recommended Routes: The Zipper (5.6), the two unnamed routes at far right end of Main Wall (5.8 and 5.9), Frog Leg Crack (5.10c), Triple Overhangs (5.10d), Triple Cranks (5.11), Credit Card Climb (5.11), Project X (5.11), Watchung Traverse (V0+/V2–).

UPPER CLIFF
The cleanest and most popular cliff.

WARNING: CLIMBING PROHIBITED—See "Access Issues" above.

1   **(V2)**   Blank slab on side of detached block which faces stream. The staircase on the left side of the start is completely off-route. TR recommended.

2   **(V0–)**   Easy south side of detached block.

3   **(6)** ★   Face route with big holds.

4   **(7)** ★   South side of pillar. Outside corners are off-route.

5   **(0)**   Chimney.

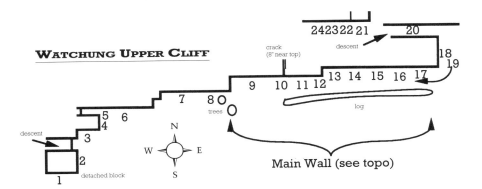

6   **(8/9)** ★   Face with crack (often wet) on left side. Hardest variation on right side.

7   **Microface (11)** ★   Face 5 feet left of tree. The outside corner and the crack are off-route. Only the top 10 feet are interesting—but they are very interesting! FTR: Jeff Gruenberg, 1982.

8   **(9)** ★   Crack behind tree. The outside corner (and the tree!) is off-route.

9   **(10a)** ★   Face with tiny overhang 15 feet above ground. Several variations possible. Usually covered with dry mud.

10   **The Zipper (6)** ★   Conspicuous 8-inch crack. Good beginner's route.

11   **(7)**   Climb face between The Zipper and right-facing corner.

12   **(7)**   Right-facing corner.

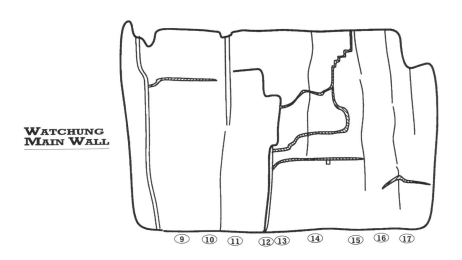

WATCHUNG MAIN WALL

13 **Triple Cranks (11) ★★**
Climb up just to right of right-facing corner. Any hold in corner or on Triple Overhangs is off-route. FTR: Jeff Gruenberg, 1982.

14 **Triple Overhangs (10d) ★★★** The best route at Watchung. Climb up about 5 feet to right of right-facing corner. A tricky sequence of moves is required to surmount the first two overhangs. Each climber seems to find a different solution. People normally use the large bucket eight feet from the top, although you can avoid this on the right for an extra pump. Down-climbing doubles the length of the route. (NJAS: Many years ago it was impressive to watch John Stannard do this route on

DOUG ALLCOCK TOPROPING *THE ZIPPER* AT WATCHUNG. PHOTO: LIZ ALLCOCK.

his first try, the first time he visited the cliff. Jeff Gruenberg once did three laps up and down without touching the ground, and then asked "When am I going to get tired?") This route has been climbed barefoot, blindfolded and unroped (although not simultaneously). FTR: Russ Raffa, 1975.

15 **Credit Card Climb (11) ★★** Climb thin seam three feet right of Triple Overhangs. Use vertical knife-blade hold just right of seam and about 7 feet up. FTR: Russ Raffa, 1975.

16 (9) ★★ Climb thin crack 3 feet right of Credit Card Climb and about 2.5 feet left of short left facing corner high up on cliff. FTR: Russ Raffa, 1975.

17 (8) ★★ Start a few feet left of right edge of cliff. Climb face to left-facing corner and follow corner and crack to top.

18 (1/2) ★ Easy south face.

19 **Watchung Traverse (V0+/V2–) ★★** Start on south face, traverse left about 150 feet and finish on final crux section above ledge behind detached block. Reverse the traverse to get a new perspective on the moves. Many variations are possible—V2- if

you traverse the crux section with your feet barely above ledge (easier if you traverse higher). This traverse has probably seen more climber man-hours than any other section of rock in NJ.

20 **The East Wall (10)**   Climb thin face on left side of descent gully. The outside corner is off-route. FTR: NJAS, 1983.

Above the main cliff is a short 14-foot cliff with some boulder problems (often top-roped):

21 **(V1)**   Climb face right of conspicuous vertical crack. Any holds that might be considered part of the crack or the outside corner and ledge to the right are off-route.

22 **Wig (V0-)**   Climb conspicuous vertical crack.

23 **(V1)**   Climb face left of vertical crack and right of small right-facing corner. Vertical crack and right-facing corner are off-route.

24 **(V0)**   Climb small right-facing corner.

LOWER CLIFF

Looser, dirtier and often wetter than the more frequently climbed upper cliff. The lower cliff takes several days to dry after rain whereas the upper cliff dries much more quickly. There is almost no worthwhile bouldering.

WARNING: CLIMBING PROHIBITED—See "Access Issues" above.

25 **(10)**   Muddy face.

26 **(10)**   Nice crack on dirty overhanging face.

27 **(8–)** ★   Crack with tiny overhang.

28 **(6)**   Nice short crack.

29 **Frog Leg Crack (10c)** ★★★   Beautiful, classic and sustained face climb starting 4 feet right of major inside corner.

30 **(7)** ★   Large crack with small overhang at top. Variation: Stay left of crack.

31 **Project W (11)** ★   Barely visible seam 3 feet right of large crack. FTR: NJAS, 1987.

32 **Project X (11)** ★★★   Conspicuous thin crack. Another lower cliff classic. Difficulty is increasing as holds break off.

33 **(9+)** ★★   Three-inch crack behind tree.

34 **(10)** ★★   Exciting loose face.

35 **(7)** ★   Large crack.

36 **(9)**   Climb face directly above right side of small platform.

37 **(9)**   Climb crack between two trees just right of small platform. Outside corner on right is off-route.

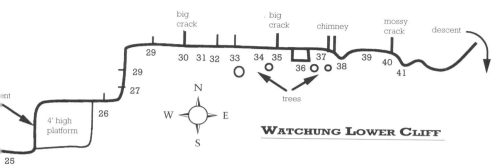

38   (8)   Crack just right of major chimney.

39   (9)   Thin crack between previous problem and large mossy crack on right.

40   (8)   Large mossy crack, often wet.

41   (9)   Crack and face 4 to 6 feet right of large mossy crack.

THE GANG AT WATCHUNG, CHRISTMAS EVE 1985: STEVE (WILD MAN) LOMBARDI, BIG DOUG ALLCOCK, JOHN MCELDOWNEY, NJAS. IN THE BACKGROUND, START OF ROUTES 14–16. PHOTO: ERIC SCHLAUGH.

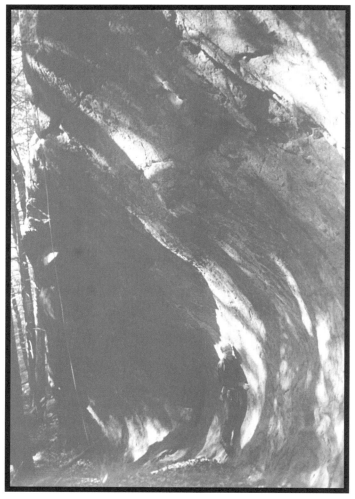

NJAS in the curl of *The Wave*, Forest Lake. Photo: Susanna Cuyler.

CHAPTER 9

OTHER NJ AREAS

The areas described in this guide represent only a small fraction of the climbable rock in NJ. We know of at least 50 other areas where climbing is at present not permitted.

But suppose the next president's only son, hang-gliding in the South-West, makes an emergency landing on an inaccessible rock tower, and, near death from thirst and hunger, is rescued by a team of climbers as hundreds of millions watch on television. In return, a grateful nation makes climbing legal (and bolting permitted) on all public property, and a commodities trader gives a casual hundred million dollars to the Access Fund for the acquisition of rock on private property. Then the following is a list of some of the best areas in NJ that we would like to see opened to climbing. Note: until these dreams come true, remember that climbing is absolutely forbidden at all of these places.

The two most exciting possibilities are listed first. The others are arranged in the same county order as the rest of the guidebook.

New Jersey Palisades; (Bergen County): Twelve miles of cliffs, up to 300 feet high, along the Hudson River. Reconnaissance shows the rock to be excellent. Climbing forbidden. Climbers have been fined and had their gear confiscated.

Passaic Falls (Passaic County): Spectacular basalt cliffs above the Passaic River in downtown Paterson. Many recent newspaper articles have described the financial troubles of this former industrial city. Opening these cliffs to climbers on a pay-as-you-climb basis could be a major source of new income for the city. Their setting would attract climbers from all over the world, and thousands of tourists would come to watch, increasing revenues at local hotels and restaurants.

Zion Boulder Field (Hunterdon County): A cluster of nice granite boulders in the woods near Zion Road on the outskirts of Sourland Mountain Reservation. Most problems are V0 to V1 but a few are more challenging. The area is believed to be on private property. Climbing forbidden.

Jugtown Boulder (Hunterdon County): This towering boulder is renowned for its powerful problems on thin overhanging faces and arêtes. It has been compared to the Mushroom Boulder at Hueco Tanks, although the resemblance is superficial. This boulder has the densest concentration of extreme problems in NJ, and would be a playground for hard-core boulderers. The height and bad landings would make many of the possibilities quite committing without a top-rope. The holds are generally very small and sharp given the steep angle, making the ability and willingness to suffer exquisite cuticle torture and devastated tendons a virtual requirement for success. At the time of writing several of the obvious lines have resisted all efforts to climb them. Unfortunately, the boulder is on private property and so this description can be nothing more than a cruel tease. Climbing prohibited.

Point Mountain (Hunterdon County): Driving east on Rt 57 from Washington to Hackettstown, this cliff can be seen (in winter) on the right side of the road. It is in the extreme north corner of Hunterdon County. The approach is by turning right on Point Mountain Rd at a traffic light 3.4 miles on Rt 57 from Washington. Bathgate's Garage is on the corner. Follow Point Mountain Rd to Musconetcong River Rd to Mountain Top Rd. The cliff is hard to locate and in any case climbing is at present forbidden.

Yards Creek Reservoir (Warren County): About 6 miles north of the Delaware Water Gap the cliffs reappear between the Upper and Lower Yards Creek Reservoirs, and reach a height of 100 feet. Private property. Climbing prohibited.

Cranberry Ledges (Sussex County): These cliffs are clearly visible above Cranberry Lake when driving north on Rt 206. Although many routes have been climbed here over the past 35 or more years, this area is on private property and at the present time climbing is prohibited.

Forest Lake (Sussex County): A couple of the best climbs in the state, including The Wave (5.10, FFA: NJAS, May 1987), are located on private property near Forest Lake. Climbing forbidden.

Edison Mine (Sussex County): On Edison Rd in Edison, a horseshoe-shaped pit, 100 feet deep, with steep rock walls, once part of an iron mine owned by Thomas Edison. The pit walls contain a large number of potential climbs of very high quality. Private property. Climbing prohibited.

McAfee Quarry (Sussex County): Just north of the town of McAfee is a dazzling white limestone quarry. This is clearly visible driving north on Rt 94, just north of the Y-shaped intersection with Rt 517. Climbing prohibited.

Playboy Club (Sussex County): Continuing north on Rt 517 from McAfee, a few hundred yards north of the intersection with Rt 94 is a private resort, formerly belonging to the Playboy Club, which has since changed hands several times. A bridle path leads right under one of the best cracks in NJ, Bloody Crack (5.10, FFA: NJAS, J. McEldowney and D. Allcock, Nov. 1985). Also on this property is a large abandoned quarry above the end of a golf course, with 60 feet high slabs. Private property. Climbing prohibited.

Crystal Springs Gorge (Sussex County): Hidden deep inside the property of a private country club on Crystal Springs Rd (off Rt 517, north of Hardistonville) is an untouched gorge, with 80 feet high sheer vertical walls. Tremendous potential. Climbing prohibited.

Mahlon Dickerson Reservation (Morris County): This Morris County reservation has good top-roping and bouldering in the Halden Lookout area. To reach this area, drive north on Weldon Rd from Rt 15 for about 4 miles, and turn left into the Mahlon Dickerson Reservation picnic area. Park and follow trail south toward Halden Overlook. The trail crosses Weldon Rd. Fifty yards beyond the road there are some boulders right of the trail, and left of the trail is the beginning of a line of small cliffs that runs parallel to the trail all the way to the lookout. The best cliff, the Cave Wall, is left of the trail about 300 yards from where it crosses the road. The trail ends at the lookout, where there are more outcrops. There are additional unexplored cliffs at the extreme northeast corner of the park, near the intersection of Weldon Rd and Sparta Mtn Rd, opposite Jefferson Middle School. Climbing prohibited.

Picatinny Arsenal (Morris County): Now that military bases are being closed with the end of the Cold War, perhaps the cliffs in Picatinny Arsenal, especially those along Lakes Denmark and Picatinny, could be opened to climbing. At present this whole area is closed to the public.

Clinton Reservoir (Passaic County): For the climber thirsty for new rock, here is a reservoir of unclimbed cliffs. At least five 50-60' cliffs line the trail along the northwest edge of the Clinton Reservoir. The north end of the reservoir is 3.5 miles north of Rt 23 on Clinton Rd. There is also good bouldering in the Hanks Brook gorge just east of the reservoir, near a bridge 2 miles north of Rt 23. The gorge connects Hanks Pond with Clinton Reservoir, and the boulders are on the right side of the gorge downstream from the bridge. A permit may be required to enter the area. Climbing prohibited.

Kanouse Mountain (Passaic County): Heading north on Rt 23, there is a rest area on the north side of the road, a quarter-mile west of the Echo Lake exit, and just before Newfoundland. At the time of writing, this rest area is closed. In past years the well-protected 5.10 crack on the boulder in the rest area has been led, and various TR routes have been climbed. Just north of the rest area are the initial cliffs of Kanouse Mountain where there are a number of climbing and bouldering possibilities, especially west of Echo Lake. Climbing prohibited.

Skyline Drive, Ringwood (Passaic County): Drive north on Rt 511 in Passaic County, turn right on Skyline Dr., and the cliff can be seen on the right at 2.8 miles. Several climbs have been done here in past years, including The Canopy (5.8) crack to overhang, traverse to vertical crack; Deadlock Dilemma (5.11a) short V-slot in 30' boulders; The Slab (5.0) 300' slab left of previous routes. Climbing prohibited.

Garret Mountain (Passaic County): The main east-facing cliffs at Garret Mountain. Up to 150 feet high, mostly excellent rock. Climbing forbidden.

Watchung Quarry (Somerset County): There is an abandoned 100 feet high quarry on the north side of Somerset St in Watchung, 200 yards southeast of the Watchung traffic circle. Much loose rock and poison ivy. Climbing prohibited.

Dead Dog Wall (Middlesex County): The abutments of the railway bridge that crosses the Raritan River from New Brunswick to Highland Park have bouldering possibilities on both sides of the river. The wall on the Highland Park side is known as the Dead Dog Wall. The dog (a black Pekinese) was found at the end of the wall by NJAS many years ago, and is safely buried. Climbing prohibited.

Ramapo Transit Cliffs (in NY, just north of Passaic County): The cliffs are clearly visible from the NY Thruway, just north of where Rt 17 joins the Thruway at Ramapo. The approach is from near the Ramapo Transit Bus Company building on Rt 17, just under the cliffs. From the fire road behind the bus company a trail leads to the base of the cliffs. People have been climbing here since at least the early 1970s, although at the present time climbing is forbidden. In the early 1980s a group of climbers including Ed Carcone, Jeff Gruenberg, Jack Mileski and Todd Ritter put up a number of routes. The crack in the obvious slab at the far left, visible from the Thruway, is 5.9+. Then, moving to the right, there is the initial overhanging dihedral (5.12 TR), then an aid route that goes through a roof, then Roof Hopper; (5.12a R, through the roofs) and Beef Hopper; (5.11d R, also through the roofs). Further to the right Sciatic Hang (5.10 R); goes through a higher roof. The named routes are all area classics. About 5 miles further north on Rt 17, the Arden Furnace; cliff near the Appalachian Trail is said to have some excellent routes. But we are getting too far from the NJ border: it is time to stop.

CHAPTER 10

MANHATTAN, NEW YORK

CENTRAL PARK
Bouldering in Manhattan!

Numerous outcrops are scattered throughout Central Park in uptown Manhattan. Near the south end of the park are three outcrops of particular interest to climbers: Umpire Rock (Rat Rock), Cat Rock and Chess Rock. These outcrops offer a number of boulder problems, some quite challenging, and all in a big city atmosphere. Countless climbers have bouldered here including the legendary John Gill.

ACCESS ISSUES   In 1987, park officials began insisting that climbers stop using Rat Rock, and some climbers were issued summons when they protested. The City Climbers Club of New York (CCCNY) was formed to work out a cooperative approach between climbers and park officials and to resolve the primary issue of liability. Among other things, members removed glass and other hazards that might injure a falling climber. Thanks to their efforts, the area is open for climbing.

DIRECTIONS   The outcrops are easily reached from Columbus Circle at the southwest corner of the park. In turn, Columbus Circle is conveniently accessed via the 1&9 subway which can be caught downtown at Times Square, Penn Station or the World Trade Center. From Columbus Circle, follow a dirt road which starts just right of Christopher's statue and heads northeast into the park. After 200', cross a paved road (West Drive) and continue straight (NE) for about 150 feet to a playground (Heckscher Playground). Skirt the playground on the left to reach Rat Rock on the north side of the playground. Rat Rock is directly between the playground and a ball field. To reach Cat and Chess Rocks from Rat Rock, head east about 200 feet to a small bridge. Pass underneath the bridge. Wollman Rink

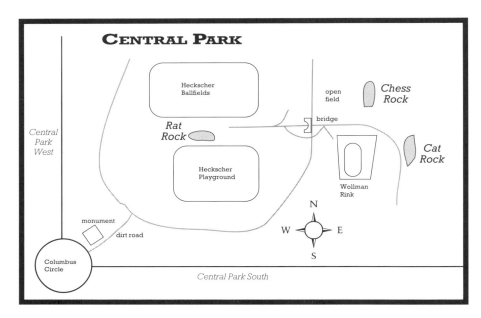

appears on your right. An open field appears on your left—and next to that, Chess Rock. Farther ahead on the east side of Wollman Rink lies Cat Rock.

(PN: My first visit to Rat Rock provided an example of the stark contrasts typical of the city. An executive-type in a dapper business suit spotted me reconnoitering Rat Rock and ventured over to explain the problems in rather excruciating detail. He regretted not having gym cloths with him but, nonetheless, removed his tie and shoes and completed a problem with bare feet. At one point, we were virtually stepping over the prone body of an oblivious homeless man who had renounced habits of personal cleanliness. I wondered whether the terrible smell might be emanating from a festering, open sore on his leg which, to my horror, seethed with a curtain of buzzing flies. I looked down to find a foothold and caught his bloodshot eyes looking at me with a kind of vacant curiosity. His eyes soon flickered shut again. I took special care not to inadvertently use him as a crash pad, thereby adding to his share of life's indignities.)

THE CLIMBING   The boulder problems are either obvious or contrived. Further information can be obtained from the locals who are only too happy to point out variations and offer advice.

UMPIRE ROCK (AKA RAT ROCK)
Best bouldering in the park. The reason for the unofficial name will become clear if you visit the area at night.

1   (V4/V5) ★   Overhanging lip traverse near right end of outcrop. Several variations.

2   (V0/V1) ★   Steep 12-foot wall near left end of outcrop. Numerous variations.

CHESS ROCK

Easy slabs and scrambling.

CAT ROCK

To the right of this outcrop are cement stairs which lead uphill. Thirty feet left of the cement stairs is a short dirt path leading to a sharp arête and corner. There are often piles of cardboard and refuse left here by homeless people.

1   (V0) ★   Left side of sharp arête.

2   (V??)   Bleak wall left of arête. Allegedly 5.13.

OTHER AREAS IN MANHATTAN

Vista Rock, located in the very middle of Central Park, just north of where 79th St crosses the park, is said to have some good boulder problems.

In the North Meadow Recreational Center there is an outdoor artificial climbing wall run by Central Park, primarily for kids. It is necessary to sign up before using it.

In the past, people have bouldered along a wall on 79th St near the Hudson River. Access situation unknown.

NJAS ON THE NEW JERSEY CLASSIC *TRIUMVIRATE.*
PHOTO: RUTHANNE WAGNER.

INDEX

This is an index of named routes and features only. Formations of areas are in all capitals.

A Touch Too Much (10 R) 45
A Year in the Life (10a G) ★★ 46
Aid Roof (4 A2) ★ 60
Ain't No Tooth Up Here (V0) 11
Almost a Problem (V0) 10
Another Start to A Year in
   the Life (10d) ★★ 46
Awkward Hawk (V0–) ★ 8
B.I.T.U.S.A. (Born in the USA
   (11 G) ★★ 44
Balance of Power (11d?) 23
BEAR ROCK 62
Big Chimney (5) 60
Bird Dog (10a G/PG) ★★ 39
BITCH BOULDER 14
Bitch Traverse (V2/V3) ★★ 14
BLACKFLY CONVENTION
   BOULDER 66
Bloody Crack (5.10) 103
Blow Out (11 G) ★ 45
Blowout (10/11) ★ 56
Body Snatcher (9) 58
Brave New World (8 G) ★★★ 72
Bulbous (V0) 16
Burnout Route, The (V0–) 8
Burt and Carole (V1– R) ★ 12
BUZZARD'S BUTTE 19
Cake Flake (4) ★ 76
CAKE WALL 47
CAT ROCK 107
Cave Boulder (V??) 30
CEDAR GROVE RESERVOIR 85
CENTRAL PARK 105

Chain Stitch (V4 R) ★ 16
Cheatstone (V0/V0+) 36
CHESS ROCK 107
Chieftain (8+ PG) ★★★ 41
Chin Chaver (10a R) 48
Chinese Handcuffs (11a) ★ 34
Class Four Ramp (1) 35
CLINTON RESERVOIR 103
Close Shave (V2 X) ★ 11
Copperhead (2) 56
Corkscrew (8) ★★★ 38
Cornercopia (V0–) 12
Count Crackula (8+ G) ★★ 73
Crack, The (5) 84
Cracker Jack (7/7+ G/PG) ★ 20
CRADLE ROCK 12
CRAIGMEUR SKI AREA 61
CRANBERRY LEDGES 102
Credit Card Climb (11) ★★ 97
Crucifixion (V0) ★ 15
CRYSTAL SPRINGS GORGE 103
Darth Vader (6 PG/R) ★ 75
DEAD DOG WALL 104
Dead Man's Curve
   (8+ G/PG) ★ 34
Death Don't Have No Mercy
   (9+/– PG) ★★★ 39
DELAWARE WATER GAP 31
Denture Grip (8 G/PG) ★ 39
Die Hard (10d) ★ 35
Direct Start to A Year in the Life
   (11d) ★ 46

Dislocator Traverse
    (V3+) ★★   76
Dog Leg (3)   54
Double Overhang (8– G) ★★   38
Doug's Roof (V2) ★   9
Down By The Corner (V0–)   11
DOWNWIND BOULDERS   64
EAGLE CLIFFS   63
EAST CLIFF   44
East Wall (10)   98
ED'S SECRET SLAB   16
EDISON MINE   102
Egg, The (V4) ★   18
Ego Hexentric (11d)   47
European Vacation
    (9+ R) ★★   45
Fannyscraper Traverse
    (V4) ★★   66
Finger Gripping Good
    (V2/V3) ★   11
First 9 (9/10) ★   57
Flakeout (V1) ★   18
Flash Appeal (11)   47
Flatulence (V0)   67
Flytrap (V0+) ★   67
Foreign Invasion (9 PG/R) ★   46
FOREST LAKE   102
Frog Leg Crack (10c) ★★★   98
Frog's Head (4/5)   55
Fusion Boots (V6)   12
Gap View Heights
    (10c G/PG) ★★   39
GARRET MOUNTAIN   104
GARRET MOUNTAIN RESERVATION
    76
Gaston (4)   57
Go For It (9) ★   60
Goldlines Are Free (3)   58

Granite Enema (V0) ★   11
GREEN POND   51
Hangman, The (7+ G)   35
Hell and High Water
    (5 PG) ★★   41
Hellacious Flake (V5) ★   62
HEMLOCK FALLS   89
Heroine Hypnosis (5– G) ★★   41
High Falls (8+ G/PG) ★★   40
HIGH POINT STATE PARK   49
Hourglass (8 R) ★   47
I-54 (V0) ★   8
Icey EB's (4)   85
In Held 'Twas I (10c)   74
In Hell 'Twas I (11b)   74
Inverse Traverse (V0+)   14
Inverted Arrowhead, The (V2)   8
IVY BOULDER   64
Jason Goes To Hell (12a?)   73
JENNY JUMP STATE FOREST   29
JG (or The Chiseler)
    (4 G/PG) ★   34
JUGTOWN BOULDER   102
KANOUSE MOUNTAIN   103
Landed Fish (V0+/V1)   8
Last Call Crack (4)   38
Leaning Pillar (4)   60
Left Corner (8+) ★★   84
Left Face (7/7+) ★   84
Left Roof (9) ★★   84
Life Is A Bitch (V2) ★   15
Little Shop of Horrors (8+ G)   34
LOVER'S PERCH   67
Lunger's Delight (V0–)   8
Mad Dog Special (6/7)   56
MAHLON DICKERSON
    RESERVATION   103

March of the Republicans
    (V0)   8
Martin's Fall (6 PG) ★   39
MCAFEE QUARRY   102
Microface (11) ★   96
MILLS RESERVATION   83
Mission Control (V2)   11
MOONCHUCK BOULDER   68
Morning Sickness
    (11 PG) ★★   41
MOUSE CRADLE BALANCING
    ROCK   68
Mouse Cradle Lunge (V2) ★   68
Mr Cohesive (9) ★   34
MT MINSI   39
MT ROSE NATURAL AREA   5
Muddy Waters (8 G) ★   45
MUSCONETCONG GORGE
    NATURE PRESERVE   22
Natural Chockstone, The
    (V0–)   8
NEW JERSEY PALISADES   101
Nick's Line (8)   60
Noisome Crack (V0–)   14
NORVIN GREEN
    STATE FOREST   69
Nose, The (9) ★★   75
Nose, The (V0+) ★   9
Nursery Clyme (V0–)   11
Old Route (4) ★   60
One Move (8)   55
OOBLIK (11d G) ★★   72
PASSAIC FALLS   101
Peace Sign (V0/V2)   9
Peanut Gallery (9?) ★★   75
Peek-a-Boo (V0–)   10
PICATINNY ARSENAL   103
PINE PADDIES: MAIN WALL   72

Pinnacle (V2)   14
Pinnacle Power (8) ★   74
PIZZA FACE   76
PLAYBOY CLUB   102
Playing House (with a Roof)
    (V0– X)   15
POINT MOUNTAIN   102
Point of No Return (9– PG)
    ★★   41
Polkacide (8+) ★   72
Pop Goes The Nubbin
    (V3 R/X)   28
Popgun Traverse (V0+) ★   67
Practice Wall (1 to 3)   72
PRACTICE WALL   49
Premature Exasperation
    (11a PG/R) ★   34
Project (V5)   74
Project W (11) ★   98
Project X (11) ★★★   98
Prow, The (V1) ★   62
Pyramid Boulder (V0-??)   30
PYRAMID MOUNTAIN PARK   61
Pyramid of Friction (V0– R)   11
Quick Access (V0–)   16
Quivering Hips (8) ★   38
Rad Dudes From Hell
    (12a) ★   38
Raincoats and Candles (7 G)   48
RAMAPO TRANSIT CLIFFS   104
Raptor of the Steep
    (10a PG) ★★   41
Razor's Edge (11a G/PG)
    ★★★   40
Red Fuzz (4)   54
REIGELSVILLE CLIFFS   20
Repetition (V1+) ★★ TR   14

RIb, The (3 PG) ★★★   38
RICKS ROCKS   41
Ride of the Valkyries (10b PG)
     ★★   36
Riding The Pig (V0–)   12
RIFLE CAMP PARK   79
Right Face (7) ★   85
Right Face Direct (10a) ★   85
Right Face Direct Variation
     (8) ★   85
Ring Ding Roof (10d) ★   20
ROADSIDE OUTCROP   68
Robbie's Route (V0)   9
ROCK JOCK'S ROCKS   10
Rockabye Baby (V0) ★   12
Rodeo (9/10) ★   60
Romparête (V0+) ★   11
Roundabout (8) ★   57
Route One (V0–/V0)   8
Salty Tears (6/7+ G/PG) ★   49
Say Your Pwayers Rabbit
     (9+ PG) ★★   35
Shin-up (V2 R) ★   15
SHIPWRECK ROCK   9
Shock The Monkey (V0)   9
Short and Stupid (V0–)   67
Short Face (5)   59
SHORT WALL   72
Shredder (V4)   9
Singer (V0)   9
SKYLINE DRIVE, RINGWOOD 104
Skywalker (12a?)   75
Slapping The Pig's Genitals
     (V1) ★★   12
Sobriety Test (7 PG) ★★   38
Son of Schnicklefritz (8)   72

SOURLAND MOUNTAIN PRESERVE
     18
Sourland Traverse (V2) ★   19
SOUTH MOUNTAIN RESERVATION
     86
Space Swing (9/10) ★   56
SPACE SWING WALL   55
Spanglish (10 PG) ★★   44
Sprout, The (3)   74
Stand, The (Project) (V??)   16
Static Cling (V2) ★   15
Stinger (V1) ★   67
Stoke the Locals (9+ R)   48
Stomach Hair Face (10c)   47
Surprise (4 P/PG) ★★   41
Swarm (V0)   67
TEETERTOWN NATURE PRESERVE
     26
Terminator (12a) ★   24
Thinner (V2) ★   9
TIC TAC TOE WALL   48
Toe (9– R)   48
Toe Dance (V0)   8
TOURNE, THE   63
Trapeze (V0 R)   11
Tree Toad Fracture (9 G) ★★   39
Triple Cranks (11) ★★   97
Triple Overhangs (10d)
     ★★★   97
TRIPOD ROCK   62
Triumvirate (10d PG) ★★★   37
TURTLE BACK ROCK   90
UMPIRE ROCK   106
Unnamed Route (3/4)   55
Vick's Fall (8)   58
Voyage of the Damned
     (10c PG) ★★★   41

War Path (11) ★   39
Warmup Route, The (V0–)   8
WARMUP SLABS   8
WATCHUNG QUARRY   104
WATCHUNG RESERVATION   93
Watchung Traverse (V0+/V2–)
          ★★   97
WATERLOO ROCKS   43
Wave, The (10)   102
Well Hung (10d PG) ★   35

WHALE ROCK   63
Wig (V0-)   98
Wookie (10?) ★   76
Wrist (4) ★   60
Yard and Ballocks (9+)   20
YARDS CREEK RESERVOIR   102
Zig-Zag (6) ★★   54
Zion Boulder Field   101
Zipper, The (6) ★   96

Access: It's everybody's concern

The Access Fund, a national, non-profit climbers' organization, is working to keep you climbing. The Access Fund helps preserve access and protect the environment by providing funds for land acquisitions and climber support facilities, financing scientific studies, publishing educational materials promoting low-impact climbing, and providing start-up money, legal counsel and other resources to local climbers' coalitions.

Climbers can help preserve access by being responsible users of climbing areas. Here are some practical ways to support climbing:

- **Commit yourself to "leaving no trace."** Pick up litter around campgrounds and the crags. Let your actions inspire others.

- **Dispose of human waste properly.** Use toilets whenever possible. If none are available, choose a spot at least 50 meters from any water source. Dig a hole 6 inches (15 cm) deep, and bury your waste in it. *Always pack out toilet paper* in a "Zip-Lock"-type bag.

- **Utilize existing trails**. Avoid cutting switchbacks and trampling vegetation.

- **Use discretion when placing bolts and other "fixed" protection.** Camouflage all anchors with rock-colored paint. Use chains for rappel stations, or leave rock-colored webbing.

- **Respect restrictions that protect natural resources and cultural artifacts.** Appropriate restrictions can include prohibition of climbing around Indian rock art, pioneer inscriptions, and on certain formations during raptor nesting season. Power drills are illegal in wilderness areas. *Never chisel or sculpt holds in rock on public lands, unless it is expressly allowed* – no other practice so seriously threatens our sport.

- **Park in designated areas,** not in undeveloped, vegetated areas. Carpool to the crags!

- **Maintain a low profile.** Other people have the same right to undisturbed enjoyment of natural areas as do you.

- **Respect private property.** Don't trespass in order to climb.

- **Join or form a group to deal with access issues in your area.** Consider clean-ups, trail building or maintenance, or other "goodwill" projects.

- **Join the Access Fund.** To become a member, *simply make a donation (tax-deductible) of any amount.* Only by working together can we preserve the diverse American climbing experience.

The Access Fund.
Preserving America's diverse climbing resources.
The Access Fund • P.O. Box 17010 • Boulder, CO 80308